Neil Peterson's determination in  and clear in *Embracing the Edge*. Reading ; the naysayers and winning against all o ir chosen path and hold tightly to their dre;

—Booth Gardner, former Governor, State of Washington

Neil does some crazy stuff, but what a super dad and role model for young people. I love his "I can do this" look at life!

–John Nordstrom, Nordstrom

Neil Peterson has led a remarkable and inspiring life, and this buoyant book is full of lessons about tenacity and daring to stretch yourself. He shows how keeping an intent focus on the goal can produce many rewards. The account is touching, funny, and full of very good yarns.

–David Brewster, author, columnist, and publisher of *Crosscut*

An intimate and moving portrait of a life full of amazingly varied jobs, health, sports, and travel experiences, including many "hard knocks" along the way. A top reading experience.

–James MacGregor Burns, Ph.D, Pulitzer Prize and National Book Award winner for *Roosevelt: Soldier of Freedom 1940-1945*

Neil Peterson lives his life the way he plays ice hockey, with a slam-bang, head-on directness, a deep faith in human nature, and the ability to see himself clearly. A man who grew up with both athletic and intellectual gifts and who has overcome challenges ranging from the ignominy of having to be rescued from the roof of the family home by the local fire department as a young man, to the loss of an eye in high school, to the demand that he agree to deliver on patronage jobs in order to be hired as a city manager (he refused and lost the job), Neil allows us to see the insights that he's gained along life's path. Throughout his primary and secondary school years, before his ADHD could be diagnosed, Neil was dismissed by his teachers as a boy who worked well above his native intelligence but who had little future in college. Instead, he was admitted to top-ranked Williams College, where he graduated with one of the most prized awards for the best senior thesis. Neil savors life with relish, and he communicates that energy and enthusiasm through his fast, engaging writing style.

—William G. Ouchi, Ph.D., Sanford and Betty Sigoloff Distinguished Professor in Corporate Renewal at the UCLA Anderson School of Management and author of *Theory Z* and *Making Schools Work*

STORIES OF TENACITY AND PERSONAL POWER

EMBRACING THE EDGE

HOW FAR COULD I HEEL OVER BEFORE I WOULD CAPSIZE?

REFUSING TO GIVE FEAR TIME TO

SO WE KEPT TALKING, METICULOUSLY PLANNING ESCAPE ROUTES AND FILLING THE TIME WITH TALK, GERMINATE AND INVADE OUR THOUGHTS—OR WORSE, OUR SPEECH.

"NO," ENRIQUE SAID, "YOU ARE COMMITTED NOW. THERE IS NO TURNING BACK."

Neil Peterson

Book Publishers Network

Book Publishers Network
P.O. Box 2256
Bothell • WA • 98041
PH • 425-483-3040
www.bookpublishersnetwork.com

To protect the privacy of individuals in the stories some of the names and identifying information has been changed.

The information in the stories are true to be best of my recollection.

All profits from the sale of the book will go to the Edge Foundation (www.edgefoundation.org), which is dedicated to helping students with ADHD by providing them with their own personal coach.

10 9 8 7 6 5 4 3 2 1
Printed in the United States of America

LCCN 2008907229
ISBN10 1-887542-95-7
ISBN13 978-1-887542-95-1

Editors: Megan Campanella, Julie Scandora
Proofreader: Carolyn Acheson
Cover Designer: Lynn Brofsky
Typographer: Stephanie Martindale

Charcoal drawing: Weagant, p 111
©iStockphoto.com

Anthony Baggett, p 33	Ben Blankenburg, p 119
Robert Brown, p 19	Daniel R. Burch, p 59
Alan Crosthwaite, p 19	Mary Marin, p 41
Denise Ritchie, p 99	

Graphic clipart © 2009 Jupiterimages Corporation, pp 41, 73, 125

Since I hope that this book will be inspirational to many, I dedicate it to the two people in my life that are my greatest inspirations—my two youngest children:

Guy Edward Peterson

and

Kelsey Edith Peterson

And to the millions of people, especially students, who suffer from Attention Deficit Hyperactivity Disorder (ADHD) and other Learning Disabilities.

Contents

Acknowledgements

What I have learned in writing my first book is that without a lot of help and encouragement, it doesn't happen.

And I have been blessed with great helpers and encouragers.

To start at the beginning, I owe a tremendous thank-you to all the people who have touched my life over the last sixty-four years. Each has in some way helped shape me, what I have done and who I am. I especially want to pay tribute to the individuals who are identified and described in the stories in this book. They not only had a significant impact on me, but they contributed to making some great stories.

This book would not have happened without the encouragement of my writing groups, one in Seattle and two in the desert (the Palm Springs area of California). When I first started to write one-and-a-half years ago, it was the feedback and support that I received from the others in the writing groups that gave me the inspiration that I needed to keep going. Thank you.

I have learned that the writer is just one small cog in the big wheel that takes a draft manuscript to be published and sitting on the book-store shelf. As a rookie in the book publishing field, I would have been lost without the help of my editors, Julie Scandora and Megan Campanella, who managed to find time before and after the birth of her first child to help. Thank you to my publisher, Sheryn Hara, who had patience and guidance when it was needed, and to my typographer, Stephanie Martindale, whose enthusiasm for the task was a joy to behold. Special thanks to my graphic artist cover designer, Lynn Brofsky, whose creative genius is only matched by her "we're in this together" camaraderie, and to Christine Cook, who was helpful in thinking through the book's structure.

Thanks also to those who kindly volunteered to read portions of the book and offer their suggestions. Established authors and friends Charlie Morris, Marsha Landreth, David Brewster, and others were very helpful with their critiques, as well as many others, including especially Nancy Chenay and Denise von Pressentin.

I also want to thank Patricia Quinn and Nancy Ratey, fellow board members of mine at the Edge Foundation, whose support, encouragement, and tireless selfless dedication have meant the world to me.

Finally, I want to thank my fellow survivors of the rogue wave—my nephew, Tim Kniffin; Tim's friend and classmate, Joe Ellis; my daughter, Kelsey; and my son, Guy—without whom I would not be here. Our experience together was the inspiration for this book.

Introduction

Off the West Coast Trail, Vancouver Island, British Columbia
June 11, 2007

*E*very ten seconds, huge rollers crash on the rocks some twenty-five feet below our precarious perch. Each breaking wave sends massive cedar logs into a frenzy, crushing anything caught between them and the walls of our cave. How long before we, too, are slammed against the rocks, giving our own to this uninhabited coast, the "Graveyard of the Pacific?"

Only minutes before, a monster rogue wave had hit us—my son, Guy (twenty-two), daughter, Kelsey (twenty), nephew, Tim (twenty-eight), and I—swept us under, and carried us into a surge channel. Constantly submerged by the incredible force of the waters, we had known not which way was up. Flailing about in the frenzied frigid sea, gasping for breath, we had won this reprieve.

But for how long? Drenched, cold, and without food or water, we shake uncontrollably. Will the five-story-high ocean cave become our tomb? The hypothermia clock is ticking.

Or will we succumb to death by entrapment? We know of no escape from this cave and the wrenching waters of the Pacific below.

I know that I must dig deep into the well of my life experiences if I am to keep us alive—to inspire us to persevere and, eventually, to survive. The stories of my life begin passing before me . . .

Graveyard of the Pacific

ONE

School of Hard Knocks

Acting First, Thinking Later

I recently read an article about a scientific study that concluded that character traits are largely set in children by the young age of three.

Boy, is this ever true. At least in my life.

I'm a risk-taker and have been for as long as I can remember. My grab-life-by-the-horns and go-out-on-a-limb tendencies of today have been with me for much—if not all—of my life.

A prime example? The day I decided to climb to the peak of my two-story house.

When I was a boy, our family lived in a fairly typical New England Georgian colonial style home in New Canaan, Connecticut: square, symmetrical in design, paneled front door in the center with a decorative crown, four windows across the front, a chimney, with an attached garage, wood siding, painted white with black shutters. And the main part of the house had a medium pitched roof.

But to a fourth-grader, the roof seemed more than just "medium" pitched. It seemed *very* tall and *very* steep…and very enticing.

Adventure called. I answered.

I started by climbing on top of the garbage cans outside of the garage. From there I was able to get up on the garage roof. I was already one-third of the way to the top! But I still had to negotiate the kitchen roof to get to the main roof of the house—the really steep one.

The kitchen, which was located between the main house and the garage, had a roofline that was lower than both the garage's and the main house's, so I jumped down to it from the garage roof. Successfully completing that second stage of my adventure, I approached the third and final stage (or so I thought), namely, climbing up onto the roof of the main house.

This was the really difficult part. I could barely reach the roof of the main part of the house from the kitchen roof, even when I was standing on my tiptoes. There was no way I was going to be able to get a good enough hold on the roof's shingles to be able to pull myself up on it. Unless…unless I used the window in my sister's room. So I stood with one foot on the ledge of the window in my sister's room and threw my other leg up on the roof of the main house. By some miracle I then was able to lift my trailing leg up—and I was on the main roof. *Voilà!*

I cautiously climbed up to the peak and carefully crouched with my legs out to either side in order to maintain my balance. Then I began to look around. I could see all the other houses in the neighborhood, and I felt as if I was on top of the world. I just rested there awhile, soaking in the good feelings from the grand view and my sense of accomplishment. I felt proud of myself. I was pretty sure that nobody else had ever climbed this roof before, and I was doubly sure that nobody *my age* had ever climbed it. I was pretty satisfied.

After a while I said to myself, *Time to get down.* I looked around and began to plot my return route. And that is where my major problem developed: I could not find a reasonable way back down. I'd gotten *up*, but I had no idea how to get *down*.

In a flash, instead of being satisfied and content with myself, I was scared to death. I froze.

After a couple of hours, my mother came outside, calling my name. She'd been looking all over the house for me.

"I'm up here, Mom"

"I'm up here, Mom," I yelled down.

"For goodness sakes, Neil! Get down right now!"

"I can't."

In desperation, my mother called the New Canaan Fire Department to come and help bring me down.

With sirens blaring, the fire truck raced up the street. And it was not just any fire truck; it was the huge hook-and-ladder truck. All the neighbors came out of their houses to see what was happening. I now had a crowd of people standing in our front yard, looking and pointing at me as if I were an animal in the zoo. I was mortified. I couldn't hide, and I knew everyone would be talking about me for days to come.

Positioned in our driveway, the fire truck extended its long ladder up to the roof of our home. One fireman then ascended the ladder and came to me. He grabbed hold of me and helped me down, carefully placing me on the ladder and then leading me down, walking backward until we reached the ground and safety.

Oh my gosh. How embarrassing.

And, of course, I got quite a talking to from my mother—and my father when he arrived home from work later that night.

Much like the talking to I'd received only the year before after a certain incident at school.

In one of my more rebellious moments, I decided to chew gum in class. And as anyone who grew up in the '50s and '60s knows, chewing gum at school was a major no-no.

And I paid for it.

Miss Higgercamp decided to make an example of me so that my fellow classmates would never be tempted to make the fatal mistake I had made. In her wisdom, she determined that I should take the gum, roll it up, and wear it on the tip of my nose for the remainder of the day for the whole world to see. Like Hester, with a scarlet "A" across her chest, I was forced to wear that wad of Wrigley Spearmint gum on my face the entire day as a sign of my terrible sin of chewing gum in school. Nor could I forget about it. Wherever I looked, that lump of gum appeared right in front of my eyes.

ONE
SCHOOL OF HARD KNOCKS

The boy who wants so badly to answer the teacher's question is Neil

So humiliating. So shaming. And exactly what Miss Higgercamp had intended.

Lunchtime was the worst. Not only did I have to face my class—I had to face the entire school since we all ate together. All classes for each of the six grades. And me, there, with a clump of gum on my nose. Needless to say, smart aleck remarks abounded.

"Hey, Neil, where's your gum?"

"Do you know there's something stuck to your face?"

"Gum nose! Gum nose!"

It couldn't get any worse for a lowly third-grader.

This trial and tribulation is so deeply etched in my memory that I even recall what was on the menu that day—Salisbury steak, one of my favorites.

The humiliation was so incredible, however, that even the promise of a good lunch couldn't keep me in line. I couldn't take it anymore, and so I bolted. I ran straight out of the cafeteria, through the school's side entrance doors, across the schoolyard, and into the bordering woods. And I kept going. I ran for what seemed like forever until I reached home, which was almost three miles from school.

Fortunately for me, third-graders are forgiving, and their memories are short. Had this incident occurred in the sixth grade, I might have been forever dubbed "Gum Nose" or some other hideous nickname. Instead, when I returned to school the next day, my public humiliation of the day before seemed to be but a distant memory for my classmates.

But Miss Higgercamp had won that round. My role as "object" in the "object lesson" seemed to have been forgotten (well, forgotten by everyone but me, that is), but her lesson stuck—no one chewed gum in class the remainder of the year, and my guess is that every single student in Miss Higgercamp's third grade class hates gum as much as I do to this day.

Both of those experiences had lasting impressions on me. To this day, I despise chewing gum.

And some fifty years later, I still carry one repercussion from my youthful climbing adventure on the roof. I never realized until

SCHOOL OF HARD KNOCKS

recently how traumatic that "small" incident had been for me. Almost every nightmare I have ever had for the last half century has me clinging to a very, very steep roof. In the dream I lose my grip, begin to slide down the roof, pick up speed, and try desperately to grab the gutter and save myself. Then I wake up, sweating like mad, and the nightmare is over.

That day on the roof, I was living on the edge—literally. And despite the nightmares that still haunt me to this day, I wouldn't have traded that boyhood adventure for the world. Anyone who's ever looked back with nostalgia at their childhood zest and zeal for life will know what I'm talking about. The thrill of pushing forward, of climbing up and up and up, even if the outcome turns out to be less than ideal, is a delicious reward in and of itself.

President of
Saxe Junior High School

Wanting the Applause

Pete Divenere was everything an eighth-grade guy wanted to be: popular, smart, athletic, and good-looking. He was a star on the football team and president of Saxe Junior High. Adults applauded him. Girls loved him. Boys envied him.

And during the second semester of my eighth-grade career, I decided to run against him for the coveted junior high presidency.

Junior high school in my district included seventh and eighth grades. In elementary school, we'd been divided between South School and Central School, depending on where we lived in New Canaan. Junior high was the first time that all of us came together into one school. In other words, it was a big deal. And running for the position of president of that school was an even *bigger* deal.

I wasn't naïve. I knew I had very little chance of winning. And I knew my opponent had everything going for him. Or, rather, he possessed the single most important attribute for winning: popularity.

What did I have? Internally, what really mattered: drive. Even then, I was a fighter. I loved competition. The fact that Pete was Mr. Everything was no barrier to me. Instead, the challenge of his standing only spurred me on. I knew I could do a better job than he—and I looked forward to proving myself.

At least that is the reason that ran on the surface. On a deeper level—one I wasn't quite ready to face at that time—I now realize that I also looked to others to affirm me. My parents who ignored me at home, perhaps—no, I desperately hoped—would finally recognize me in my school achievements.

I also had experience. I had served as the president of my homeroom in seventh grade and as student council representative for my homeroom in seventh and eighth grades.

But externally, my biggest advantage had nothing to do with holding elected positions or having familiarity with the workings of student government and everything to do with getting elected. Again, winning was a simple matter of being known by the most students. And I had the perfect position for exactly that: I was lieutenant in the school safety patrol.

The school safety patrol existed to ensure that students were respectful and orderly as they traveled from class to class. Safety patrol members were stationed on the stairs in between class breaks to make sure that none of the kids pushed or shoved each other or ran in the halls.

I was lucky enough to get the primo safety patrol assignment. I was stationed at the landing between the first and second floors in the main hallway. Wow! Every single day, more kids passed by me than they did anyone else.

Of course, just being in a spot where all *could* see me didn't guarantee that all *would* see me. After all, most students ignored those "eyes of the teachers" and focused on their friends they were walking with. This is where who I was entered the picture. Later in high school, I would get the nickname "Sunshine," but in junior high I was already well into the bubbly personality responsible for the name. I was friendly, but I was also brazen. I stood in my choice position and smiled and said "hi" to everyone I knew who passed by me. What an opportunity! I saw everybody, every day, and they saw me.

But a pretty face and a bubbly personality weren't enough to win the votes of those who didn't even know my name. And that's where the third key to my advantage came in: Kim Kelly. Kim, accomplished and creative beyond her years, was the girl who served as my campaign manager. For the all-school assembly, she made a poster board presentation that was incredible. I still have it to this day.

It was masterful, it created a "buzz" about my candidacy, and it filled the one missing piece in my campaign. To those who didn't know me, it gave a name to that person standing on the landing every day saying "hi." Now everyone knew who Neil Peterson was. Thanks to Kim, I now had, as they say, good face and name recognition going into the election

Election day came and...I won! I couldn't believe it. I beat the incumbent! The best-looking guy in the school! The star athlete! I was ecstatic!

I couldn't wait to share the news with my parents. I was thrilled that on that special day, for some reason, my parents came to school to pick me up. (I usually rode the bus.) I ran out of the school with my books in my arms and jumped into the car, yelling, "I won! I won! I won!"

My parents' reaction was unbelievable. They turned around in their front seats, put forefingers to their mouths, and said, "Shhhhhh!"

I was devastated.

In my moment of great joy, I felt utterly alone. Knowing that through my own efforts and planning and determination I'd defeated the guy who "should have won," I desperately wanted to share my victory with those closest to me and to hear them say that, yes, I'd done a great job. Yet the two people I had most expected to cheer with me had turned their backs on me.

All I could do was think, *What had I done wrong? What in the world*, I wondered, *did I have to do to get their approval? What more did they want?*

Even though a majority of the school had voted for me and had celebrated my success, my own parents would not even acknowledge my victory. I can't even say that, given the opportunity to vote, they

Kim Kelly's poster board presentation

PRESIDENT OF SAXE JUNIOR HIGH SCHOOL

He held the office of President last year in Miss Anderson's seventh grade homeroom.

Neil is a trustworthy, helpful, loyal, friendly, courteous, kind, obediant, cheerful, thrifty, brave, clean, reverent, and hungry Boy Scout.

As you all know Neil is a Lieutenant on our beloved Traffic Squad.

Our boy has had a seat in the Student Council for the last two years.

Neil has a good brain for all things. For the last two years he has had an A- average.

All this good experience plus a shining personalty makes a good leader. Don't you think so?

would have voted for me. And in my eyes, their two votes were the only ones that counted. Why couldn't they applaud me?

In my campaign, I had learned what I could accomplish with sheer determination, some experience, choice opportunity, and effective support.

But in my victory, I had learned a very different and sobering lesson: When I needed support, I would have to look beyond my parents. Applause would have to come from elsewhere.

THREE

The Classics

Learning How to Learn

My prep school required that every boy take Latin. This requirement had a long history to it. Studying Latin was the tradition in East Coast prep schools, which were modeled upon the English "public schools" (i.e., our private schools) that believed it was part of the foundation of a well-rounded and superior education. This thinking also had some validity. Latin serves as the base for several romance languages such as French, Spanish, and Italian, making the study of those languages easier or, at least, giving familiarity to the meaning of many of their words. And since 60 percent of English words are derived indirectly or directly from Latin, its study would help with word derivation in my own language. Also, many of our grammatical rules stem from Latin. And some believed that SAT scores were higher the more Latin that you knew.

Over the years, this requirement has changed. Now you hardly ever hear of students in high school taking Latin.

The requirement at The Taft School was for only one year of Latin, but I signed up for *four* years. I even took another year of Latin in college.

My Latin teacher was John Small, Mr. Small to me. He was a long-time Taft teacher, a confirmed bachelor, and a bald, hard-driving coach of the track and wrestling teams. If there was anybody who could make Latin interesting it was Mr. Small. He was a great teacher. He was also the one who first gave me the nickname of Sunshine.

More unbelievably, I signed up for and took four years of Classical Greek.

Several reasons contributed to that decision, but only one really mattered.

First, I was told that Classical Greek would be very helpful to me later in life, especially in the derivation of words. I would be able to figure out what words meant even though they were new to me. So I was told.

Second, I was told that if I took the equivalent of a Classics major (both Latin and Greek), I could be excused from the requirement to take biology. This was good news for me because I had no interest in biology.

And then there was the real reason. I had heard that the teacher of Greek was the best teacher in the school. I wanted to take a class from him, no matter what he taught, just to see what a great teacher could do.

Evidently, not many other students thought as I did for on the first day of my freshman year when I entered the Classical Greek classroom, I noticed a very empty room. There were only four of us.

So, three other thirteen-year-old freshmen and I had the best teacher in the school all to ourselves. Our classes were fifty minutes long, and we met every day except Sunday each week. That's right. We met on Saturday, too!

Over the years we read the top poets and their most famous works, including Ovid's *Metamorphoses* and Virgil's *Aeneid,* as well as Homer's *Iliad* and *Odyssey*—all in the original Latin and Greek.

My Greek teacher was Robert Woolsey. Mr. Woolsey would later go on from Taft and become the Headmaster of the Casady School in Oklahoma City for seventeen years.

Arma virumque cano, Troiae qui primus
ab oris~Italium, fato profugus, Latin lavini
aque venit~litora, multum ille et terris
iactatus et alto~vi superum saevae memo-
rem Iunonis ob iram; multa quoque et
bello passus, dum conderet urbem, infer
retque deos Latio, genus unde Latinum,
Albanique patres, atque altae moenia
Romae. Musa, mihi causas memora, quo
numinae laeso, quidve dolens, regina deum
tot adire labores impulerit. Tantaene ani
mis caelestibus irae? Urbs antiqua fuit, Ty
ryii tenuere coloni, Karthago, Italiam cont
ra Tiberinaque longe ostia, dives opum
studiisque asperrima belli; quam Iuono
fertur terris magis omnibus unam post
habita coluisse Samo; hic illius arma, hic
currus f
si qua fa
fovetqu

Learning the classics

Suffice it to say that he made Greek so interesting that I continued to take it for all four years that I was at Taft. I loved the classes, even though the subject was hard for me. But he was a terrific teacher, and he inspired me to want to learn more, to work hard, to tackle something that I knew nothing about. He got me to learn how to think, to analyze. He helped me gain confidence in myself. He helped me become an enthusiastic learner.

Mr. Woolsey's written comments about my performance during this period were laced with accolades: "Neil's record in this course represents hard work, conscientious attention to responsibility, and a desire to do well unmatched by any other in this particular class." In short, he inspired me and acknowledged my resulting efforts.

Have I ever used this knowledge that I acquired at such a young age? Hardly. But that was never the impetus behind my taking Greek. Instead, I experienced excellence in action under Mr. Woolsey. And from him I became a lover of learning.

Yes, Latin and Greek have helped me figure out what some words mean, but only a few.

Yes, Greek studies did help me figure out what fraternity or sorority someone was in, since I knew the Greek alphabet.

Yes, in my travels, Latin and Greek have helped me read the sayings in certain stained glass windows. But, no country, including Italy and Greece, is using the classical languages in its everyday speech. Modern Greek, for example, bears very little resemblance to Classical Greek.

Only once has my knowledge of Classical Greek been used extensively and made a difference to anyone. This instance happened, of all places, on Chappaquiddick Island, where my family used to summer.

For some reason, an amazing number of ministers of many faiths vacationed on Chappy during the summer. Each week some fifteen or so clerics would get together in the evening at one of the group member's summer homes. Word got around that I knew Classical Greek, and they asked me if I would be willing to come to their meetings to read the New Testament from the original Greek to them. I responded, "Sure."

They welcomed me with open arms. They were so excited to have a chance to listen to me read to them from the original text. I only hoped I would be up to the task. I was only sixteen at the time and not sure I could meet their expectations. But I started. I began to read out loud to them. I silently read the original words in Greek but translated them out loud into English for my audience. And, wow, what a revelation! We were all amazed at how different the original meaning was from some of the translated versions that are on the market that most people and most ministers use.

What I was doing was perfect for the ministers because it gave them additional insight into what the original words of the New Testament meant. From this they could craft their sermons.

They loved it, and I loved doing it. We met and read and translated and discussed all summer long.

Although that experience was gratifying in allowing me to use my knowledge, I benefited in other ways from my studies. Learning the Classics—Greek and Latin—was a challenge, but it was a rewarding challenge. I traveled that academic path for personal reasons, not for outward appearances or to impress others, and in the end, I had a healthy sense of pride, of accomplishing something I never would have thought possible.

I learned from Mr. Woolsey that is largely what mentors are all about—leading others into accomplishing what they never would have thought to tackle on their own. And that is precisely what Mr. Woolsey did in helping me navigate through two languages I never would have thought to try learning.

In the process, he not only taught me Greek and Latin; he also taught me to simply love being taught. I discovered the joy in learning for its own sake. To this day I continue to be an enthusiastic learner.

FOUR
Skating at Night

Putting in the Hours

Like most prep schools in the '50s and '60s, the one I attended, The Taft School in Watertown, Connecticut, was single-sex, and it required that each boy play a sport during each season—fall, winter, and spring.

Although I was not a star athlete, I was a competitor from the get-go. The challenge of the contest and the camaraderie of the team (my "family" substitute) appealed to me.

So, for the fall of my freshman year, I went out for football—and won the starting quarterback position on the team. To put this in perspective, the best freshman football players were playing on the varsity and junior varsity teams; I was playing on the sophomore and freshman team.

The coach for this team was Len Sargent, who also happened to be the varsity hockey coach. Hockey at Taft was king—it was much more important than football.

Toward the end of the football season, Coach Sargent told me that he wanted me to play ice hockey in the winter. I told him that I had never played and that I had skated only a few times.

"I don't care about that," he said. "I have a team just of freshman and sophomores that are selected, in part, because of their future potential. Perhaps even to play varsity hockey."

My basketball skills weren't very good anyway, so I said to myself, *Why not?*

The tryouts were *very* difficult. Considering I could barely skate, I didn't think I stood a chance next to the other boys trying out for the team.

But surprise, surprise—I made the team. Albeit as fourth-line alternate. But I made it. Nobody could believe it. It created quite a buzz around campus; it just didn't make sense that *I* had made the team and others who were much better hadn't.

The only thing I can figure is that Coach Sargent saw a special spark in me that compensated for my lack of experience, and that spark was drive. I was determined to be a great hockey player, and I greedily grabbed at every opportunity that would help me realize my goal.

In my freshman year, for example, I was struggling with learning how to skate—much less how to stick handle and score. So, to get additional ice time to practice my skating, I would sneak out of my dorm room late at night, after lights-out, and walk to the rink in the dark and cold with my skates in my arms. The rink was at least a fifteen-minute walk from the dorm—uphill.

Once I got to the rink, which was locked and dark, I would scale the side walls to get inside. (The rink at that time was covered but not fully enclosed since construction had not been completed on the side walls; so it was possible, albeit difficult, to climb into the rink even though the doors were locked.)

I would then lace up my skates and get on a completely dark rink, with maybe a little moonlight shining in, and skate and skate and skate. Nobody ever saw me do it. And to this day, I have no idea if anyone ever knew. But I didn't care. I was skating for one reason and one reason alone: purely to improve myself for the team.

Sophomore year I made it to the first line of the same team. My junior year I advanced to be the starting defenseman for the junior

Fourth-line alternate

varsity team. And in my senior year I was one of the regular defensemen on the varsity team. I was never the star, but I was the hardest worker and hustler on the teams.

Coach Sargent never said anything about my nightly winter forays and probably didn't even know what I was doing, but part of me thinks he wouldn't have been surprised. During the football season, he had looked beyond physical appearances and seen my enthusiasm, my hunger for improvement. And, above all, he knew he had a competitor who loved the challenge.

Coach Sargent (far left, back row), Neil (fourth from left, back row)

FIVE

The Glee Club

Turning Rejection into Success

Incredibly, The Taft School's student body, four-hundred-boys strong, was taken with the idea of singing. At least they gave that impression—a far cry from what you'd find in most high schools, then or now. Because in my day, Taft was an all-boys boarding prep school. The only way to meet girls was to join the Glee Club, a boy's on-campus singing group that would often give concerts at girls' schools in the area.

As a result, almost every boy in the school joined a singing group.

There were two singing groups on campus. Besides the Glee Club, the "cool" singing group was the Oriocos, a group of twelve boys who sang at events throughout the school year. They were the best singers in the school.

I tried out for the Oriocos but unfortunately didn't make it. I don't know why I even tried out. I had had no experience singing prior to then. But, what the heck? I'd had no experience with hockey, and look at what had happened. Why not singing, too? So I suppose I shouldn't have been surprised that, although I wasn't accepted to the Oriocos, I was one of the last boys cut. *Not bad*, I said to myself. *I almost made it.*

Then came tryouts for the Glee Club, for which everyone tried out—and into which everyone got accepted. Nobody ever got cut.

As I said before, the best thing the Glee Club had going for it were the concerts at the girls' schools. The boys would dress up in tuxedos and practice their music first. Then the girls, all in beautiful dresses, would get on the stage and practice theirs. Then there would be a concert, with the boys from Taft and the girls from whichever school we were visiting singing to the audience. After the concert there would be a dance—and of course that was what all the boys looked forward to.

Since everyone made the Glee Club and since I'd already done so well for my Oriocos tryouts, I knew I'd have no problem making it into the Glee Club. Well, to my shock, I was cut!

I couldn't believe it. Nobody ever got cut from the Glee Club! I was outraged, discouraged…and particularly upset about the impact this would have on my being able to see, meet, and dance with girls. (Let's face it: I didn't care about the singing.)

I really wanted to go to the girls' schools on the weekends, and I wasn't about to let the Glee Club's decision interfere with my planned social life. My anger and upset quickly turned into creative energy. And I got an idea, a brilliant idea.

The director of the Glee Club was George Morgan, a very old music teacher. He'd been at Taft forever and was getting on in years. Although music may have moved him, he probably didn't enjoy all of the physical work his job required at that stage in his life.

I went to Mr. Morgan and asked him if he could use a manager for the Glee Club—someone to set up the folding chairs for the practices, someone to pass out the sheets of music, someone to do the grunt work.

Well, he said he had never considered having a manager before, but now that he thought about it, it would be very helpful. He said "yes."

And so, as a thirteen-year-old freshman, I became manager of The Taft School Glee Club. And I would serve in that position for the next four years because I sure as hell wasn't going to give it up. It was heaven!

Somebody has to set up the chairs and pass out the music (Neil, front left)

First of all, I got to go to every concert at every girls' school.

Second, I was allowed to wear a madras sports jacket, which in those days was cool, while the other Glee Club members were stuck in their tuxedos, all looking like cloned penguins.

Third, I alone got to mingle with the girls while the Taft boys were on stage practicing for the concert to come.

Fourth, I had a degree of authority, something of great value. Very quickly, other boys on campus started coming up to me to ask if I needed some help in my duties. Could they be an "assistant manager" so that they too could go to the concerts and dances? In fact, by the time I was a senior, I had five assistant managers working for me. Needless to say, I didn't have to set up many chairs myself.

And finally, when it came time to apply to college, I put on my resume,

Glee Club, Manager – '58, '59, '60, '61.

Guess what? The colleges thought this meant I was "musical" and "well-rounded." They never guessed the true story.

In rejecting me, the Glee Club had given me the greatest gift. I received the opportunity to create a dream job and get what I really wanted—contact with girls. I even got an added, unsought-after bonus of prestige and power.

And I didn't have to sing a single note.

SIX

Academics at Taft

Ignoring Limiting Labels

I'm a Winston Churchill fanatic. For the last decade, I've read everything I can get my hands on that has been written either by or about him. I spent a month in Great Britain in June 2008, visiting Churchill historic sites, learning details of his life, and absorbing a sense of the greatness of the man through the places he lived and worked.

Why am I so fascinated by Churchill? Because I can identify with him. Many scholars today believe he had Attention Deficit Hyperactivity Disorder (ADHD). If this is true, then Churchill, like me, struggled through his school career with undiagnosed ADHD.

In many ways, our lives were incredibly similar. We were both handfuls as boys, brimming with energy and prone to turn to humor and pranks when not sufficiently challenged. We both sought the approval and attention of our parents, especially our fathers, who showed little interest in our school activities or academics. We both balked at authority, transferring the anger we held for our fathers toward other authority figures. We both hated taking tests, often did poorly on them, and consequently struggled getting into schools because of poor results on placement tests.

We did have our differences. Churchill was terrible in math, while that was my best subject. He was a voracious reader, while I struggled to read because of my dyslexia. He blossomed academically in college, while I started to shine in high school.

Nonetheless, despite these differences, I strongly identify with Churchill. His academic experiences especially resonate with me for we both overcame negative assessments to achieve success beyond predictions.

My educational struggles started early, from the time I began elementary school in the 1950s. My report card for Miss Eddy's sixth grade class typified my academic record: mediocre. Although I was "alert to current happenings" in social studies and "participate[d] wholeheartedly in physical education," two areas in which I received E (for "Excellence"), a solid 75 percent of my grades were S (Satisfactory), and some fell into the dreaded I (Improvement Needed).

Even more striking were my grades in "development of attitudes and habits," an area in which a poor student could excel (he's not very smart, but at least he tries hard). The grades here tilted even further into the "just okay" and "needs improvement" realm. My report card also shows that my parents requested conferences with Miss Eddy.

In junior high school, I continued to struggle, but I was able to do homework for extra credit, which I did with a vengeance.

But when I began my high school career at Taft, there was no longer the opportunity to do extra credit work to raise one's grade. Plus, I was competing against some very smart and talented boys. There were only about eighty in my class, so we made a close-knit and competitive group. Yet, surprisingly, my academic record improved tremendously. Despite the increased challenges—or maybe because of them—I began receiving outstanding marks.

During my freshman year, for example, I ended up with an average of "Honors" grades, and placed fifth in my class. The following year I continued to excel, placing ninth in my class.

It's clear to me, looking back, that my hard work and determination were to thank for my performance. At the end of my sophomore year, Taft's venerable headmaster, Paul Cruikshank, sent my parents a letter informing them of my class standing and commending me

Winston Spencer Churchill

for my "hard and conscientious work." Yet his praise was somewhat backhanded, noting that "since [Neil's] aptitude for things scholastic, as revealed by several tests we have given him, is not on the high side, Neil deserves double credit."

Teacher comments were along the same line—full of praise for my hard work and performance yet denigrating my achievements by pointing out my lack of "natural" intellect. "In spite of having only an average aptitude for the subject," one math teacher wrote to my parents, "Neil was able to join the 'fast' algebra section well into the year, make up the work that he missed, and attain an excellent average throughout the rest of the year.

"He may very well have more difficulty with the work in the 'fast' section next year," he continued. "If he doesn't 'make a go of it,' it surely will not be for want of trying, and I am equally sure that he will make an excellent record in a 'regular' division if it becomes necessary for him to drop back."

All of this concern over my intelligence reached a crescendo in February of my junior year when Mr. Cruikshank called me into his office.

To be called into Mr. Cruikshank's office was not a good thing. A tall, slim man with an elongated face and prominent straight, stern nose, Mr. Cruikshank was a man to be feared. "Shank," as we called him behind his back, always dressed in a suit and never took off his jacket. He wore glasses, only occasionally removing them—and only then when it was to pierce you with his eyes so that you were sure to remember the point he was making. He had been headmaster of the school for 25 years, the only other headmaster in the school's 71-year history since Horace Dutton Taft, the school's founder and brother of the twenty-seventh president of the United States. The man was the quintessential headmaster. He didn't have a funny bone in his body.

My visit to his office that day was a first for me. What I discovered was a dark, daunting room. On the wall behind his desk hung a huge, somber portrait of his predecessor. Opposite his large wooden desk and his own high-backed chair were just two other seats, black captain's chairs with The Taft School insignia on them. The windows, eight leaded panes to each, were so ancient that the glass, wavy from

"Neil, in the scholastic area you have some limitations" —Headmaster Paul Cruikshank

the effects of gravity over the years, gave a distorted view of the world outside.

At Mr. Cruikshank's bidding, I took a seat in one of the captain's chair. Mr. Cruikshank cut to the chase.

"Neil, as you advance in grade here," he said, "you will discover that plain hard work and determined effort do not produce the results they did in the lower grades. As you doubtless know, your aptitude on the verbal side is below our average here. This means that the more advanced work of the junior class—where dealing with ideas, more imagination, more ability to analyze, to organize, etc., are needed—is proving to be more difficult for you, and your good efforts don't produce the results and grades they used to. And this will affect your ability to go to the college of your choice."

I sat on the edge of my chair and straightened my back.

"Sir," I responded, "why am I always being judged by my aptitude test results? They may not be accurate. In any case, it is quite unfair that low aptitudes should militate against a boy's admission to college."

Mr. Cruikshank didn't seem to be in the mood for debate. He simply reminded me that life is unfair sometimes, that reality isn't always ideal.

"Neil," he concluded, "I am afraid that you're going to have to face up to the realization that your studies are difficult for you, and in the scholastic area you have some limitations."

When I left his office, I felt as if I had been whipped.

My parents told me shortly thereafter that they'd received a letter from Mr. Cruikshank recounting the conversation. He'd written, "This is doubtless hard for a boy of Neil's ambition and determination to accept philosophically without suffering an ache or two."

Mr. Cruikshank was right. It *was* hard for me to accept the prognosis that I simply wasn't intelligent enough—so accept it I did not. Winston Churchill once said, "Never, never, never, never, never give in." And I did NOT. I refused to live by the "sub-par intelligence" label that Mr. Cruikshank and everyone else wanted to me to wear.

Instead, I worked doubly hard.

When the corridor master called "lights out" every night, more often than not, I pulled the covers over my head and turned on my

"Why am I always being judged by my aptitude test results?"

flashlight so that I could get more studying in without his knowing that I was still up.

I was driven to succeed in part because I was told I couldn't—because Mr. Cruikshank assumed I was working too hard to make up for my lack of intellect and because my parents believed him. I wanted deeply to win the recognition and approval of my parents, especially my father.

Even more important, I was able to succeed because I found some teachers who believed in me, challenged me, and connected with me emotionally.

My favorite quote, which is attributed to Winston Churchill, is, "Success is all about going from failure to failure without losing your enthusiasm."

Ultimately, this is why I was able to succeed at Taft. Throughout elementary and junior high school, I'd had more than my fair share of failures, including less than perfect marks and report card comments about my poor behavior, yet my enthusiasm never waned. I kept plowing forward, enthusiastic as ever.

The result? A can-do attitude that allowed me to succeed, even when academics became harder than I'd ever experienced before. Many around me suggested throwing in the towel, acknowledging that I was less gifted academically and just not able to "cut it" in the competitive academic arena at Taft.

But my gut told me otherwise. It told me to persevere, to push through the nay-saying and reach for my goals.

And in the end, I'm so glad that's what I did.

I made the honor roll many times at Taft. And many times, my name was posted on a small sign outside of the headmaster's office—located in the most heavily trafficked corridor in the school—identifying the top three students in each class for each month.

But the greatest accomplishment of all was simply achieving what others thought impossible for me. In attaining what Cruikshank and my parents assumed to be out of my reach, I tasted the sweetest success of all.

SEVEN
Circumnavigating
Chappaquiddick Island

Setting Personal Goals

I have always looked for adventures, for challenges, for opportunities that would test my mettle. I love a contest, not just to win—or to try to win—but also to set standards against which I can continue to improve upon.

One summer on Chappaquiddick, at the age of sixteen, I decided that I would do something that nobody had ever done: circumnavigate the island alone, and being the first, set a world's record for doing so.

Chappaquiddick Island sits off the main island of Martha's Vineyard. It is bounded by the Atlantic Ocean to the south, Nantucket Sound on the east and north sides, and Edgartown Harbor on the west side. The total circumference of the island is nearly eighteen miles. Chappy, as it is commonly referred to, is approximately six square miles in size, not counting Pogue Pond and its wetlands. With only about two hundred year-round residents and with fewer than five hundred homes, Chappaquiddick, which means "separated island" according to the Chappaquiddick Tribe of the Wampanoag Indians, prides itself on being separate from Edgartown on Martha's Vineyard, although technically it is part of the town. Chappy is reachable only by the On Time Ferry, which is a barge that can carry three cars and several bikes and goes back and forth across Edgartown Harbor all day long. At times it is also possible to get to Chappy from the "mainland" of Martha's Vineyard via four-wheel-drive vehicles on the sand spit barrier beach that, depending upon the weather and storms, often extends across Katama Bay, the southerly end of Edgartown Harbor.

My sailing vessel for the excursion would be a sailfish. Invented in the early '50's, the sailfish was essentially a large wooden surfboard with a sail, rudder, and dagger board. It was the precursor to today's sunfish, the major difference being that the sunfish has a well for your feet that is self-bailing. Another big difference between today's sunfish and yesterday's sailfish is that today's version is made out of fiberglass. The sailfish is the simplest boat to sail ever invented and the most popular, having sold more than half a million over the last fifty years. Almost fourteen feet long and four feet wide, today's sunfish weighs 130 pounds.

My sailfish was one of the early ones, old, wooden, a heavy 150 pounds, and only ten feet long and three feet wide. It was given to me by a neighbor on the island. It had been getting dusty, just lying in his garage unused. First thing I did was clean it up. Then I gave it some pizzazz. Over a background of black, I painted bright red and orange flames starting in the bow and extending down the hull of the boat for four feet.

And, of course, I gave it a name. I called it Blazer.

Most significant to me was that it was mine. And it worked.

I loved sailing it in front of our house, especially on high-wind days. I probably tipped over a thousand times. But I didn't care. Naturally, I got completely soaked. But, hey, it was all about the challenge. Each outing presented a new experience with different lessons to learn. How tightly could I head into the wind? How far could I heel over before I would capsize? How far could I lay out, gripping onto the mainsheet for dear life, before I fell over backwards into the water?

Blazer

With all of that practice close to home, I needed to expand my sailing horizons. A circumnavigation of the island would put those lessons to the test and involve far more challenging problems.

To successfully navigate, my planned adventure would take some preplanning, some strength, a lot of endurance, much perseverance, and some luck. My trip would be in four parts. Traveling clockwise, I would first go directly east to Pogue Pond and second head south in Pogue Pond, ending up in Poucha Pond after having negotiated the narrow stream connecting the two ponds. The third part would include two substantial portages and a short but dangerous westerly sail in the Atlantic Ocean along Wasque Point (pronounced WAYCE-kwee). The final and fourth segment of the trip would be the long northern run from Katama Bay up Edgartown Harbor. Besides mapping out my route, I had many variables to take into account. As the sole sailor on my watercraft, I would be fully responsible for paying attention to the wind, both its direction and velocity. Equally crucial for my negotiating the open waters would be my knowledge of the tidal flows and currents.

On the big day in the middle of the summer, I was up early, all excited in anticipation of this amazing adventure. What a challenge. Of course, my parents thought that I was nuts. But they always thought that. And I didn't care. I was determined to circumnavigate Chappy solo and do it in record time.

Shirtless, no sunglasses, and with only a swimsuit on, I pushed off from the beach in front of our house at 8 a.m. sharp. It was a beautiful sunny day. Luckily I had a good breeze coming out of the north. I wanted a good wind because the stronger the wind the quicker the trip. And I needed speed to set the world's record in this event that I hoped would remain intact for decades beyond.

The northerly wind allowed me to sail a beam reach directly east. I did not have to tack once for the first three miles along the north coast of the island. This water body is commonly referred to as Edgartown Harbor but is technically part of Nantucket Sound. It is the home of all the Edgartown Yacht Club sailing regattas. If I kept on this heading, I would eventually end up on Nantucket Island. But before I knew it, I entered the "gut," a very narrow opening that led into a huge bay called Pogue Pond, which takes up a large portion of the eastern part of the island and extends three-plus miles, or almost half the distance of East Beach, which makes up the eastern border of the island.

I was relieved to enter Pogue Pond because it was protected from the wind and waves and because it was a body of water I knew intimately since we had rented a house there for years before buying the house that we currently lived in. Also I knew that entering the pond represented the first milestone for what was to be a very long and demanding day.

With the picturesque Cape Pogue Lighthouse in the distance, the northerly wind flow was a blessing. Shortly after entering Pogue Pond, I turned the tiller of the sailfish so that the sailboat was facing south, and I planed with the wind at my back. I let the mainsheet out as far as it would go, the large sail at right angles to the hull of the sailfish. While this is exhilarating, the boat gets very tippy with the sail so far out to the side.

I passed many of the coves where I had clammed for years. I passed by my friend Brad's house. And I headed toward the far south end of the pond, which is connected by a stream to Poucha Pond, which in turn is very close to Wasque Point, a full seven miles from Cape Pogue Lighthouse. The stream connecting Pogue Pond with Poucha Pond is a serpentine, very shallow wetlands that winds for more than two miles. To navigate this in a sailboat would be a trick and a half.

Again I was amazed at how lucky I was to have a trailing wind and ecstatic about the time that I was making.

Entering the stream, which is part of the Cape Pogue Wildlife Refuge, was difficult because of the sediment build-up from the runoff of the wetland into Pogue Pond. I had to lift up my dagger-board to prevent it from getting stuck in the white sandy bottom, only one and half feet deep. Luckily I had enough momentum from the long run downwind that I got over the sandbar and into the creek bed without having to walk the sailfish.

Next a new test. The creek was narrow, anywhere from twenty feet at the widest to as little as only ten feet in others. Tacking in such a confining channel when my sailfish was only ten feet long would be difficult. But because of the trailing wind, my job became a lot easier. Still I had to work every minute, pulling the mainsheet in and letting it out on the other side to allow the wind to steer the boat along the sinuous stream.

The other lucky break was that the tide was coming in, and therefore the current was going in the same direction that I wanted to go. If either the tide had been going the opposite direction or if I had been heading into the wind, my chances of negotiating this stream with the sailfish would have been almost impossible.

But I had other trials still to come.

Ahead of me I could see the bridge, the infamous wooden Dyke Bridge, now popularly known as the Kennedy Bridge as a result of the tragic drowning of Mary Jo Kopechne on that fateful night on July 18, 1969.

The height of the mast of my sailfish was a good five to six feet taller than the bridge, yet somehow I would have to go underneath the very short opening that the bridge provided. I planned to take down my mast and sail and boom for just enough time to get underneath and through the bridge and then put the mast back up. This plan was challenging because I had to do it while I was underway. I had to have enough momentum so that the tidal flow would allow the sailfish to float under the bridge and not lose steam and get stuck there.

While the sailfish was moving toward the bridge, I stood up and lifted the mast out of its recessed six-inch-long holder. At the same time, I grabbed hold of the boom, the sail, and the mainsheet without their falling into the water and then kneeled down while the boat went under the structure, all without losing my balance on basically a board on water. And I did all of that while keeping the sailfish on a heading that went right through the middle of the opening and avoided hitting the pilings of the bridge on either side. The opening was only ten feet wide. And the channel was way too deep for me just to get off the sailfish and walk it through the overpass' opening.

Once successfully past the bridge, I reassembled the mast, boom, sail, and mainsheet and headed to the last portion of this section of the adventure—namely, Poucha Pond.

This would be one of the most arduous sections of the trip. I had to get the sailfish and all of its rigging from Poucha Pond over the sand to the Atlantic Ocean and Wasque Point. I would have to portage. The sailfish was much too heavy for me to carry. Instead, I would have to drag it, holding on to the cleat on the bow, and pull it over the sand dunes one step at a time. And I would have to be careful where I stepped in the sand because the entire point is protected and in trust, including the piping plovers that make their nests in the sand.

At that point in the day, the sun was blazing. The sand was even hotter. And my feet were bare and about to be burnt with every step I would take. The distance I had to traverse was about four hundred feet, or the equivalent of a football field and then some. That section of the island was—and still is—very deserted. There was no one to help me.

I began to question why I was doing this.

What made me concerned was that the most dangerous part of the journey was just ahead: launching the sailfish in the Atlantic Ocean and surviving the dangerous currents and undertow at Wasque Point.

I was nervous. I was scared. And I was alone.

I also had no food or water or protective clothing, just my swimsuit.

Nevertheless I forged ahead, pulling the heavy sailfish one foot at a time over the searing sand dunes, straining with each step I took. I had to stop every few minutes because my feet were burning from the hot sand. I would stand on the sailfish to give my feet a break. Then I would pull a few more feet until I could not take the burning of the soles of my feet.

While the first three parts of the trip (reaching Pogue Pond, sailing downwind in Pogue Pond, and negotiating Poucha Pond and the connecting stream and bridge) all went perfectly and seemingly quickly, this fourth section took forever, and it was exhausting. I was not sure that I would make it.

Somehow I did.

Exhausted, sunburned, famished, thirsty, I stood on the beach at Wasque Point looking out at the forbidding ocean. Because of the bottom configuration and the way the currents merge at the point, the waters there always seem to be boiling, roiling in rage. No one swims there. No one goes sailing there. The only users of this section of the shoreline are the seagulls, common terns, and American oystercatchers looking for food and a few surf-casting blue fishermen with their rods set on the front bumper of their jeeps, patiently waiting for a bite. The place is forbidding, even in the middle of a bright sunny day.

I stopped to collect myself. I thought through how, once I set the sailfish into the ocean, I would sail it along the shoreline without getting caught in the turmoil of the conflicting water currents at Wasque Point. I was in the lee of the wind, which would make getting a good wind to power me through the difficult stretch of ocean more difficult.

At last, I'd had enough waiting and wondering, and I launched my sailfish into the surf of the ocean, paddling with my arms to get it out beyond the breaking waves so that I could set the mainsail by pulling the halyard and tying it to the cleat at the base of the mast. This is not easy when you are being knocked around by waves.

Finally I got the rigging in place, held on to the mainsheet, pulled it in tight to try to capture the wind, which was now coming from my right, from the north, hoping to create enough speed to be able to sail along the beach. I wanted to be far enough out so that I would not get caught in the breaking waves but not so far that I would have any danger of getting caught in the roiling waters of Wasque Point.

The contest was that the wind was not as strong as I would have liked because I was so much in the lee of the wind. I begged the sailfish to go faster, but it just moved at its own pace without seeming to listen to me. I made progress but ever so slowly and painfully. The mainsail luffed a lot in the wind, every once in a while catching a gust and moving me forward a little. Oh boy, would I be happy to get out of the ocean and into Katama Bay, the southernmost part of Edgartown Harbor, for the last leg of my journey.

After what seemed like a long time, I reached a point along the sandbar that sometimes connects Chappaquiddick Island with the main island of Martha's Vineyard. "Sometimes" I say because whether the sandbar extends that distance depends on the ocean, that year's storms, and the tidal action. At the time of my voyage, the connection was complete, which meant the second of my portages.

I dragged the sailfish out of the ocean onto the sandy beach so glad that the shortest but most dangerous portion of my trip was over. I sat on the sand, contemplating my circumstances. I was more than half way and had conquered the most difficult sections of the trip. That was the good news.

The bad news was that I still had two major tests in front of me. One, I would have to portage the sailfish over the sandbar to be able to launch it into Katama Bay. Second, ahead I would have a very long sail straight into the wind to get from the south end to the north end of Edgartown Harbor and close to my starting point.

The second portage was shorter—only 150 feet—than the first, but just as difficult. Slowly I struggled, battling my exhaustion, the relentlessness of the hot sun, my burning feet, and the heaviness of my sailfish.

Finally I launched in the water of Katama Bay, an area that I was familiar with because I musseled there in the Boston whaler. Just as Pogue Pond had been my favorite spot for clamming, Katama Bay, at the very south end of Edgartown Harbor, was my favorite spot for musseling. The blue mussel, which is also a member of the bivalve mollusk family, with its pearly shell, is wonderful to eat when simply steamed in a half-inch of water. As I relished the thought of some mussels for dinner, I reminded myself that I had had no food for the last seven hours. I was hungry, and my body was sending signals of impending starvation. I had no electronic gear on board to call for assistance, and momentarily I imagined a sailor on the bridge of a destroyer with his Navy signal flags frantically sending a message that I needed food: Foxtrot, Oscar, Oscar, Delta.

That thought quickly passed on. I needed to get back to the task at hand. I would have to tack the entire way up the harbor, a distance of five miles, watching out for the many boats anchored or moving about in the harbor.

Edgartown Harbor presented quite a sight. Beautifully maintained white clapboard homes lined the western shore of the harbor. Hundreds of boats large and small rested at their buoys in the harbor, each turning with the wind in the same direction. Dinghies and the Edgartown Yacht Club launch popped in and out, ferrying people to and from their boats. Fishermen were repairing their boats, preparing for the next day's efforts. Sailors were cleaning off the salt spray after having spent several hours enjoying the fresh breezes of Nantucket Sound. Yachts were being cleaned and prepped for a stunning sunset evening cruise. And in the midst of all this activity, a little ten-foot sailfish madly tacked its way through the larger-than-life boats and anchor ropes and buoys to make it back home in world-record time.

After spending three hours tacking in between the yachts of Edgartown Harbor, I finally reached the main section of Edgartown with its restaurants, yacht clubs, fishing charters, hotels, and churches. A beautiful New England town of only three thousand year-round residents, Edgartown calls for walking as the only practical way to get around the downtown. The few streets are very narrow, all one-way. The town police once stopped me for going the wrong way (backwards) on a one-way street. I argued with the police officer that I was facing in the correct direction, but that argument did not win the day.

I passed the Edgartown Reading Room, to which my dad belonged. But I never fully understood the purpose of the group or what happened at meetings. All I knew was that it was an honor to belong and my dad did not go over to the reading room to read. Beyond that I knew nothing.

Next came the Edgartown Yacht Club, to which our family belonged and where we ate once a week. It also held occasional dances during the summer.

I sailed by the Chappaquiddick Yacht Club, which was a tiny shed of a building. My dad and several others founded the organization on Chappy as a kind of joke. It was really an excuse for a party

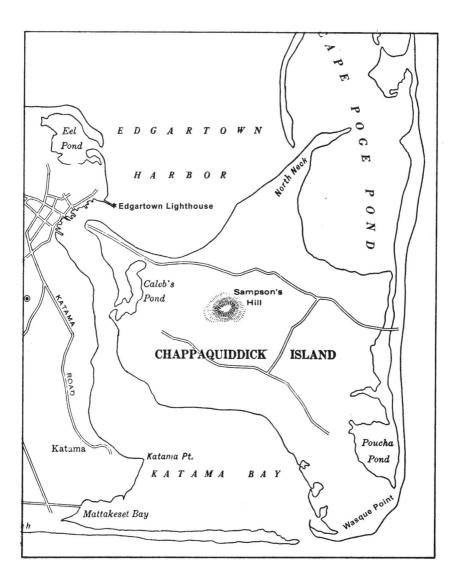

Chappy

and a parody on the Edgartown Yacht Club and all of its rules and nautical protocols.

On my port side I passed the town's public pier from which a small crowd of tourists would invariably gather in the early mornings (7:30 a.m.) of the workweek to watch me paddle my rowboat from Chappy across Edgartown Harbor. I had to oar my way across because the ferry did not start running until much later. And my rowing created a spectacle because I did it in a business suit with pant legs rolled up and shoes and socks off so that they would not get wet from the casual water that always seemed to be in the bottom of my rowboat. Needless to say, nobody on Martha's Vineyard wore a business suit, let alone wore one while rowing. Except me, thanks to my summer job on the Vineyard as a bank teller.

And I passed the On Time Ferry, which was the lifeline for those of us living on Chappaquiddick Island. The three-car ferry went back and forth for fifteen hours every day, and the crossing took a total of three minutes. When I passed it, John waved to me. John was the owner/operator and a fixture to all of us who lived on Chappy. At the stern, John was all business, focused on dodging the watercraft making their way into and out of Edgartown Harbor. Deep lines marked his weathered face from the constant exposure to the elements. Seasoned and salty but with a glint in his eye, John saw everybody and everything that came on and off Chappaquiddick Island. I liked John; we got along.

Once I saw John's face, I smiled broadly because I knew that I had made it. I knew that I was nearly home, and I felt a tremendous sense of accomplishment. The classic and striking Edgartown Lighthouse, the symbol of the entrance to Edgartown Harbor, was directly in front of me. As I left the harbor behind me, I was able to see my parents' house for the first time in eleven hours. I sailed with the wind coming from my left, from the north, as I passed the Chappaquiddick Beach Club and followed the coastline for another mile to our house.

I had done it!

My parents and sister were on the beach waiting for me and relieved that I had returned safe and sound. But I could tell from their expression that they were also thinking, *Why? What in the world possessed you to do this? You must be crazy.* I knew they didn't understand, but at least my parents had let me make the trip.

Only I could savor the satisfaction of what I had done. Dog tired, roasted by the sun, and famished—but more important, invigorated, stimulated by the challenge, and satisfied with my accomplishment.

As far as I know, my journey, which took eleven hours and twenty-three minutes, is the world record for the circumnavigation of Chappaquiddick Island. I believe it still stands to this day: To my knowledge, no one else has even attempted to circumnavigate Chappaquiddick Island in a sailboat.

✳ ✳ ✳

I wonder, *Why is this story is so meaningful to me?*

The answer eludes me. No official contest drew me. No real Guinness World Record was at stake. No crowd of friends and well-wishers urged me on.

Why did I take on this adventure? And why would I remember it in such detail and for so long?

Maybe what makes it special has to do with the very fact that there was no outside force or reason for it. The expedition was entirely self-driven. The desire came from within. My inner self wanted to do it, set up the challenge, and make it a contest. And in the end, I alone realized the accomplishment, relished it, and took satisfaction from it.

I did it for myself and not for anybody else. And maybe that is OK.

EIGHT
Seeing Clearly

Gaining Insight from Loss

"Neil..."

I could barely hear my mother; she was practically whispering. She placed her hand on top of mine.

"Neil, there's something I need to tell you."

"Okay. What?"

I didn't like how she was behaving. Something was wrong, worse than...

"Neil, the accident...um...well, honey...you're never going to see from your right eye again."

"What do you mean?" I asked, jerking my hand away from hers. "That I'm blind out of that eye?"

"No, Neil...you lost the eye."

"What do you mean I *lost* the eye?"

"It's gone, Neil. The injury was so great that they had to take the eye out. And the bones around the eye were broken too."

I couldn't believe it. I had been in the hospital for almost a week and was just now finding out? Why hadn't anyone told me?

I flopped back against my pillow, looked at the ceiling, and expelled all my air in one hot, angry sigh. Why hadn't they told me? I pounded my fists on the mattress and was silent for minutes. I could see I was scaring my mom. *Good*, I thought. *How dare they not tell me.*

"Why didn't you let me know sooner?" I finally demanded. "Why didn't the doctor tell me?"

"We thought it was best for you if we let a few days pass first," she answered softly.

I turned my head away from her and stared at the wall.

"I'd like to be alone now," I said.

I heard my mom gather her purse, then leave the room. Then I tried to make sense of what had happened over the past several days.

✳ ✳ ✳

A week before, I'd been with my best friend, Phil Livingston. We'd been golfing at the New Canaan Country Club. There was nothing unusual about that. Phil and I had been best friends since seventh grade, and we did almost everything together, including sports. Our favorite summertime sport was tennis, but occasionally we would take breaks to go swimming, eat a hamburger and fries, or play golf. That day had been one of our golf outings.

We had been on the second hole, the one right on the corner of Country Club Road and Smith Ridge Road, where passersby in their cars could see us tee off. My drive had hooked to the left, landing in the deep rough on this challenging par-four hole. Phil had teed off next. His drive had been even worse than mine—and it had made him mad. He had started swearing and pounding his driver on the ground.

While he had carried on, I had grabbed my bag of clubs, swung them over my right shoulder, and proceeded to walk down the fairway to find my ball, all the while contemplating my strategy for getting out of the rough and back on course. Suddenly I had heard a *swoosh* and a *thwhack*. I had swung around—and met Phil's golf ball square in the right eye. Without my knowing, Phil had decided to tee off again.

I didn't remember a whole lot after that point, other than a few snatches from the ambulance ride to the hospital.

Next I had woken up in a hospital room. My mom had evidently been keeping vigil, sitting in a chair across the room, reading a magazine, a pillow and blanket by her side. She was forty-three, but she looked older, her salt-and-pepper hair framing her round, prematurely wrinkled face. In her twenties she had been a model; now, slightly overweight and aged beyond her years, those days were long gone.

A nurse had been beside me, adjusting my IV drip.

Only I hadn't seen her immediately.

She had stood right beside me, just two feet to my right, but I hadn't known she was there until the sound of her tossing a medicine vial into the garbage can had jarred my attention toward her. And that's when I had realized something was wrong. I had strained my neck, shifting my entire torso to see that woman who stood directly beside me.

Then I had understood: I couldn't see out of my right eye.

The nurse had shot me a saccharine smile, having finished her duties, and trotted out of the room.

Why can't I see out of my eye? I'd thought. I had slowly inched my fingers up my face, starting at my chin, until I had come across what felt like a bandage. I had let my fingers follow the outline of the gauze; it had covered my entire right eye, bulging like a baseball from my cheekbone to my eyebrow, from the bridge of my nose to the right side of my face.

My mom had still sat there reading, unaware that I had woken.

The memory had hit me fast, and then a horrible wave of nausea had washed over me. *They must have bandaged up the eye to keep the swelling down*, I had thought, continuing to finger the bandage on my face, trying to bring back what couldn't be retrieved.

I had cleared my throat so my mom would know I was awake.

She had put down her magazine and quickly crossed the room. "How are you feeling?"

"Where am I?" I had asked.

"Stamford Hospital," she had responded gently.

"What time is it?"

"11:30 in the morning."

"What happened?"

"You were brought here from the country club. They performed an operation on your face—on your eye. They had to sedate you. You've been asleep since yesterday evening."

Just then the door had opened, and a doctor and two nurses had entered my room. He was not my usual doctor. This doctor was tall, with short hair and glasses and dressed in the typical knee-length white doctor's coat. He had held a writing tablet in his left hand.

"Well, young man, how are you doing today?" he had asked as he came to my side. His familiar tone had made me uncomfortable. He had spoken as if we'd already met and become best of friends. Then I had remembered that I'd been out of it for at least twelve hours; technically, he had met me before.

"Okay," I had responded, but I was certain he caught the hesitancy and anxiety creeping into my voice. I had felt far from okay, either physically or mentally.

"Let's take a look at how you're doing," he had said, drawing closer. He had cautiously peeled the bandages off my face, one layer at a time. After what had seemed like five minutes, he had finally finished. He had pulled a flashlight out of his doctor's coat and shone it into my right eye. I had strained to see the light…strained *so hard* to see that light.

There must be more swelling than I realized, I had thought because I couldn't see anything out of that eye.

"How does it look?" I had asked the doctor.

"Okay," he had answered, "but we need to keep this bandaged up a little longer. You take it easy, Neil, and I'll see you again tomorrow morning. Okay?"

"Okay," I had responded. "Thank you, Doctor."

He had left the room, and the two nurses had attended to me, re-bandaging my eye.

The doctor had repeated this checkup for several days. Each morning, and sometimes in the evenings, he would visit, light in hand, and take a look at my eye. And each time I would try hard to see that light, but it was always the same. Darkness. Nothing but darkness.

Two days after my admittance, Phil had visited me. He had come with his parents, who had chatted with my mom while Phil and I had caught up.

"Hey, buddy," Phil had said, crossing the room. He always called me "buddy." "How you feeling?"

"Ahh…I've been better."

Still best friends, Neil and Phil

"Yeah, I can imagine," he had said. There was an intensely awkward pause. "Look, man, I'm really sorry... I don't know how that happened, and..."

"Don't worry about it, Phil," I had interrupted. "Really. It'll heal up."

"Yeah...," he had awkwardly replied. No wonder he had looked doubtful. At the time, I had chalked it up to his guilt about the accident, his wishing he could undo injuring his best friend.

I hadn't held it against him then. I could understand his guilt. I remembered thinking at the time that, if our roles had been reversed, I would have felt just awful for having given my best friend a humdinger of a black eye like mine. And now? I guess I still didn't hold anything against him. If I had caused him to lose his eye...wow... I didn't know how I'd be able to handle that.

But I sure didn't know how *I* was going to handle *this*. My eye...gone!

✳ ✳ ✳

At that point in my life, I cared tremendously about how I looked and how I performed at sports.

Most of the time, I thought I was a pretty good-looking guy, reasonably appealing to girls, and a pretty good athlete. At least, I tried to believe that. But deep down, I doubted it. I wasn't sure I was attractive, wasn't really sure girls liked me, and thought I was just average in sports. These were all typical adolescent insecurities, and although they may seem trivial to adults, they mean the world to a teenager—how others view him and how he fits in with his peers.

But the one thing I *did* know at this point in my life was that although I wasn't the *best*-looking guy and I didn't have the *most popular* girls seeking me out and I wasn't the *star* athlete, I could certainly try my hardest to compete for all three. And try I did.

But now, this news that my eye was gone—*gone!*—seemed to shatter any chances I had. It was as if the bottom had fallen out of my life strategy. As I sat in that hospital bed in the days following my finding out the truth about my eye, I became painfully convinced that it wasn't even worth trying anymore, that I should simply give up my attempts to be the best at the things that mattered to me. I felt completely hopeless.

When I finally did get home, things seemed to get worse. I was back in my "normal" surroundings, but nothing about my life seemed normal anymore. Every time I looked in the mirror, a bandaged face met my gaze. When I reached out to pick up my glass of milk at the breakfast table, or tried to shake someone's hand, or went to turn a doorknob, I would miss. With one eye gone, my depth perception vanished, and even simple daily tasks were no longer simple.

My peripheral vision suffered, too. In the first few weeks following my return home from the hospital, I was constantly running into things on my right side.

One of the most heart-wrenching experiences for me was trying to regain my skills in tennis, a sport that I dearly loved. I would go to the hitting board—a practice area where a person could hit the tennis ball against a backboard, eliminating the need for a partner—and practice for hours on end. Sometimes I would hit the ball perfectly, but more often than not, I would be slightly off in my timing. The ball would arrive at my racket a tad too soon on one hit, a tad too late on the next. But still I kept at it, determined not to let the loss of my eye translate into a loss of my tennis skills.

Off of the tennis courts, however, I was not a determined fighter. I was bitter, angry, and depressed. I felt that I'd been dealt a cruel hand, and I spent much of the summer as a recluse, avoiding time with even my closest friends. Late in the summer my parents took my sister, my grandmother, and me to Chatham, on Cape Cod, as a way of cheering me up. My dark mood continued, and finally my parents decided they had had enough. They told me flat out that it was time I got over the accident, that I started being decent to others, that I "grow up."

Although their words may well have been spoken more out of their own frustration than selfless love, they got my attention. I realized my parents were right; I *did* need to change. I couldn't stay in that funk forever. I decided then and there that I was going to take charge of my attitude and stop acting like a victim. It was several months before I found myself fully following through on that resolve, but nonetheless, the wake-up call I got that week in Cape Cod was pivotal.

✳ ✳ ✳

In September I returned to Taft to resume my schooling. Being among so many others—peers as well as teachers—was hard, as I'd grown used to a summer alone. Now, every day I had to go to three meals in the dining room with four hundred other boys. Every day I had to walk the hallways between six different classes, passing hundreds of boys along the way. And every day I had to sleep and study in my dorm room on a corridor with many other boys. From morning till night, I felt as if every single boy I ate with, passed in the hall, or spent time with in the dorm was staring at me, looking at my eye. I was still dealing with depression over my summer's trauma—and here, at Taft, it was impossible to be the recluse I'd been at home.

Nonetheless, I didn't stay in that dark spot forever, and I attribute much of my emotional recovery to my willingness to stay involved in sports, even though that had challenges of its own. Despite my injury, I had never even debated in my mind whether or not I would continue to play sports competitively. I would. Period.

I tried out for varsity soccer that year. As I prepared for the try-outs, I was determined to make it. I knew that if I made the team, it would give me the sense of normalcy I craved, of returning to my pre-accident existence. "You can do this," I told myself. "You can move forward, Neil."

But when I got on the field, I knew I'd been naïve. Things were still going to be tough—and different. The biggest difference was the mask I now had to wear, which had been custom-made for me. It was big, awkward, and embarrassing. In many ways it made my vision even worse. Negotiating my way down the field was doubly hard. But I stuck with it. I went to every practice—and I made the team.

I was so proud.

This wasn't to say all my trials were gone. Most of the boys at Taft were nice to me, but when I traveled to compete against other prep schools in soccer during the fall and hockey in the winter, I suffered a lot of hazing and ridicule. Of course, the opposing teams and their

*The truth is I can see the world—and myself—more
clearly with just one eye*

fans had no idea what had happened to me. They only saw that I wore a big, black, slit-eyed facemask—and that nobody else did. Their favorite chants were "the masked marvel" and "Hey, Lone Ranger, where's Tonto?"

But despite it all, I have often said that the accident was the best thing that ever happened to me. Why?

Because that accident forced me to stop trying to be the best looking, the most popular, the greatest athlete. It allowed me to begin just being myself—and to try to *enjoy* being myself.

Before the accident, I was a poor sport with a horrible temper. I would get all worked up over the smallest mistakes I'd make on the field or on the rink. After the accident, I felt something I had never felt before: the sheer joy of playing.

Just being out on the field competing was reward enough. All of a sudden, it was not so much about being the star, being the best athlete on the field, or scoring the most goals. No, it was about the thrill of just being on the field, running with my teammates, touching the ball occasionally, and playing my heart out.

And today I'm proud of the fact that I can be competitive in a wide variety of sports, even if I'm not "the best" at any of them. I carry a respectable 5.3 handicap in golf—not bad considering that I have no depth perception whatsoever. Yet I'm able to keep things more in perspective than I did before.

I still try to look handsome, still try to woo the girls, and still try to be better in every sport that I play…but relative to what I was like before the accident, the difference is night and day. The accident changed my life dramatically—and all for the better.

By cultivating an honest and, at times, painful humility in my life that I wouldn't have come by any other way, the accident has allowed me to identify with people in my life who have disabilities of their own. It has even taught me how to empathize with friends and family when they experience loss in their lives—different kinds of loss, but loss nonetheless. And it taught me about forgiveness.

The truth is, I can see the world—and myself—more clearly with just one eye.

NINE

Hockey at Williams

Taking Charge of One's Fate

Hockey is big at Williams College. Being a smaller school, Williams doesn't have the following that the well known Division I colleges and universities do that are perennial contenders for the NCAA College Final Four in ice hockey, schools such as Boston University, Boston College, Denver University, the University of Michigan, among others. And, as a Division III college, Williams puts less emphasis on sports than on academics compared to Division I institutions.

What Williams lacks in numbers of spectators or level of funding for sports it makes up in enthusiasm. The majority of students fill the stands for home games, and significant numbers of professors, alumni, and even townspeople join them. Sports do play an important role at the smaller colleges such as Williams. With only two thousand students, Williams has consistently been selected by *Sports Illustrated* as the number one Division III college in the nation for its sports program.

Hockey's following on campus may have something to do with the long, snowy and cold winters in northwestern Massachusetts. Students, faculty, and townspeople look for entertainment and reasons to emerge from the comforts of their homes as well as outlets to vent their pent up frustrations.

And hockey, in particular, is a great sport to watch. It has almost nonstop action with a lot of hitting. It's fast. It's thrilling. And it's a tremendous adrenaline rush for players and fans alike. Williams has historically fielded some decent teams. It has a good tradition of playing quality hockey and winning.

For all these reasons, hockey is big at Williams College and was just as important in the fall of 1961 when I arrived for my freshman year.

And it was big for me too. Having played at Taft, one of the premier hockey prep schools in the East, I was eager to play at Williams. I loved the sport, and my competitive nature led me to try out for hockey when I arrived at Williams.

The hockey coach was a no-nonsense guy, very serious on the ice. He was always on his skates, pushing each player to expend more effort. Very self-effacing, with a wonderful sense of humor off the ice, Bill McCormack coached the Williams men's varsity and freshmen hockey teams for thirty-five years. He was revered at Williams. The Coach's Trophy, selected annually for the best coach at the college, is named after him. He served as president of the American Hockey Coaches Association, was selected "Small College Coach of the Year" by the Eastern College Athletic Conference, and was chosen New England Coach of the Year in 1961-1962.

Back in the early 60's, freshman were not allowed to play varsity sports. So most colleges had freshman teams in almost every sport, as Williams did in, among other sports, ice hockey. But the freshman team was important as the training ground. Coach McCormack knew this and took a real interest in the freshmen team; he knew that the best players on it would be playing on his varsity team next year.

After two weeks of brutal tryouts, Coach McCormack, or just "Coach" to us, announced the team, and I was selected. He quickly started to put together his lines and defensive pairings. His first line consisted of Gary Burger, Sam White, and me.

The next fall during rush week, the Kappa Alpha fraternity indicated that it would like to have me join its team. This was reaffirming

Freshman first line—Neil, Gary Burger, Sam White

because this frat house was known as the hockey house, with most of the varsity hockey players as fraternity brothers.

So when I tried out for varsity hockey in the fall of my sophomore year, I saw all the signs pointing toward my being selected. My two line mates and I were the top freshman line, and that line usually became the varsity team's "sophomore" line. And as a member of the hockey fraternity house, others on campus obviously recognized me as a varsity hockey player.

The tryouts for varsity were arduous, as was to be expected from Coach McCormack. I clearly understood that the talent on the team was tremendous and, if I made it, I would hold a position only as part of the sophomore line, possibly the third line, but more likely the fourth line on the team.

As usual on the final day of tryouts, the coach brought each one of us into his office to tell us the news about whether we had made the team or not. When my turn came, I went into his office. Coach McCormack was not comfortable in this setting; his workplace was on the ice. The room looked as if had never been used. He sat behind a gray metal desk with nothing on top of it. In the office there were no calculators, no mimeograph machines, nothing but a phone. No pictures on the walls. One light in the ceiling. I sat down in the only other chair in the room. It was wooden with arms on it. I sat forward, a little nervous—no, very nervous—hoping and expecting the coach to tell me I had made the team as a sophomore

Making the team was very important to me. I really wanted to play varsity hockey. I loved the sport, and I loved the competition. And I wanted to be around the guys on the team.

The coach looked me straight in the eyes and said, "Neil, you are a terrific kid. A coach cannot ask more from a kid than what he gets from you. You give 120 percent every time you are on the ice. You had a good freshman year last year. Your work ethic is unmatched. Your attitude is excellent. Your enthusiasm and hustle are an inspiration for the other guys on the team. You are not going to be the high goal-scorer or the most talented playmaker, but you bring a passion to the rink that infects everyone else. You should be proud of that. And you are a pleasure to coach. You listen to what I say and try to implement the suggestions that I give you."

"Thanks, coach," I replied. Oh boy, I was feeling good and becoming more relaxed. Everything he said I knew to be true. But hearing someone whom I admired so completely actually say it to my face meant a lot. I felt great.

"But, Neil, I have some bad news for you."

"What?" I asked. My face contorted in amazement.

"You are not on the team. It was a tough decision, but there were so many good players that there just is not room for you. I'm sorry. I'm really sorry."

I could not believe it. I was stunned. My mouth all of a sudden felt parched. My eyes welled up.

"Coach," I said, "why? Why would you break up our line? Why?"

His head bowed down a little, and then he raised it back up. "Neil," he said, "it is because of your eye. Playing hockey is too dangerous. We just cannot take the chance that something could happen to your good eye. It is too risky. I am so sorry."

I could hardly speak; I was so overcome with emotion and utter disappointment. I wanted to leave before he saw me cry, so I said, "Thanks, Coach," and turned and left the room in a hurry.

I was devastated. Not only did I love playing hockey, not only did I love being around the other players on the team, but I also loved having hockey represent something much deeper to me. In part, it defined who I was—not necessarily to others but to me. And it represented the results of my hard work and persistence, all those long hours of practice at Taft and after. The achievement that it represented for me was great because I had started skating and playing hockey only in ninth grade, when most other hockey players had been playing since they were little kids.

Playing hockey also came at a time when I was reevaluating myself and life. I was going through the sophomore blues. Or maybe it was the beginning of a sophomore slump. I was reading Rollo May's *Man's Search for Himself.* I was writing like mad in my journal, trying to figure out what was important in life. On top of the turmoil within as I came to grips with who and what I was, events outside me were churning. The college was going through a huge change as it had just announced that it was going to be eliminating fraternities on campus.

And then this. I was embarrassed, totally humiliated. Everyone knew I had played first line on the freshman team. Everyone knew I had tried out for varsity. Everyone expected me to make it. How could I ever explain this? How could I face my line mates? How could I face my fraternity brothers, many of whom were on the varsity hockey team?

I walked and walked for a long time, trying to make sense out what had happened.

The juxtaposition was too much. On the one hand, Coach had told me that I was an inspiration to the team. On the other hand, he had cut me from the team.

Because of my eye.

After I had lost my eye three years earlier in the freakish golf accident, I made a commitment to myself that I would not let that accident set me back. In fact, I had resolved that I would work even harder to accomplish what I wanted. I needed to show myself and others that I could do whatever I set my mind to achieve. And the most obvious stage for this comeback of sorts was the athletic field. That was where I had performed at a high level before the accident, and that was where I had received most of my feedback in life. That was where I had created the foundation for my self-image.

To have come back from the horrible loss of one eye to play varsity hockey at The Taft School was a major achievement for me and one for which I was very proud. I knew that I was not the best player on the team by far, but I was so proud just to be on the team. To continue to play hockey at Williams affirmed my resolution made those three years before.

I could not let this setback deter me. I refused to accept the decision without giving my all. I'd done as much for the tryout, and now I needed to do the same for what appeared, to me, to be an arbitrary and unfair decision. So the next day, I went down to the ice rink after

"Coach, practice at the usual time today?"
Coach McCormack (back row, left), Neil (front row,
second from right)

class and sought out Coach McCormack. I asked if I could talk to him. He said "sure," and we walked to his office.

Before either of us sat down, I spoke, "Coach, I have thought a lot about what you said yesterday. I want to play varsity hockey at Williams. I want to play for you. I know that my eye is a concern for you, but I believe that the decision on whether to risk injury should be mine not yours. I'm the one who has to decide whether I'm willing to take the risk of playing. I'm the one who will have to live with the consequences. I should be making this decision. Coach, I want to play."

Coach McCormack, standing, blinked his eyes more than once. I could see that he knew the overwhelming emotion behind my words. His eyes were beginning to well up.

"Neil," he said, "you're right. It should be your decision. If you want to play, you're on the team."

I could hardly find words. Turning my head so Coach could not see my tears, as I left the office, I said, "Coach, practice at the usual time today?"

"See you there, Neil."

One Hundred Doors

Refusing to Settle

"**M**r. Peterson? You can see the congressman now."
I fumbled for my briefcase, scooped it into my arms, and quickly stepped around the receptionist's desk into the room where she motioned.

It was the spring of my sophomore year in college, and I was trying to line up an internship on Capitol Hill for the upcoming summer. I'd been lucky enough to be selected for a fellowship that would pay living expenses for an entire summer in Washington, D.C., as long as I found an intern position. So here I was, interviewing for a congressional internship in our nation's capital.

My excitement mixed with trepidation. An internship with a congressman meant I could see what congressmen did, day in and day out, learn how the political game was performed in D.C., and hopefully, have some fun too! But I also felt an intense pressure in living up to the expectations of the fellowship; I had been one chosen out of hundreds of candidates. And I felt a bit fearful in facing the nation's leaders who weren't scared of anyone and probably had no time to talk to a college kid.

Fears aside, I was set on finding a position. I had decided that Washington, D.C., in the summer would be great. I couldn't wait to explore all the museums, the monuments, the night hangouts—and to have some good runs. I had already decided that my regular jogging route would be from the Capitol building, down the mall to the Lincoln Memorial (where I'd take in the Gettysburg Address, of course), and back. History and athletics: In my mind, there couldn't have been a better combination.

The receptionist flashed a pleasant smile and then closed the door behind me, leaving me alone in an office with my first job prospect: my own home-state congressman, U.S. Representative Ab Sibal.

Congressman Sibal was a liberal Republican, representing the Fairfield County area of Connecticut. He was serving his second two-year term in Congress, having been elected from a district which, at the time, was very Republican, although it also included the Democratic stronghold city of Bridgeport and several communities that served as suburbs of New York City. Up to that point in time, Congressman Sibal's district had *never* elected a Democrat to Congress.

In my eyes, working for Congressman Sibal would be the perfect internship for me. He was somewhat liberal, which fit with my political beliefs at that time; he had been in Congress for a while, so he wasn't a rookie; and, most importantly, he represented my home district. This was important, because I had some political ambitions of my own. Working for my home congressman was a perfect arrangement, allowing me to learn the ins and outs of the district that I hoped I might one day represent.

Congressman Sibal came out from behind his desk, shook my hand, and asked me to take a seat on the couch while he settled into a chair opposite me. He wore a dark, slightly rumpled suit, and glasses were perched on his round face. The chair he sat in was large, but he filled it all.

"So, where do you go to college, son?"

"I'm attending Williams College in Massachusetts, sir."

"And how long have you lived in my district?'

"For most of my life."

The U.S. Capitol

"And your major is…"

"Political science, sir. I'm majoring in political science."

The congressman sat just a few feet away, but the coffee table between us could have been the Grand Canyon. He seemed distant, aloof, as if he were eager to get through this interview so he could move on to the next thing on his plate. I didn't blame him; I knew he was busy. But at the same time, something just felt "off." I had hoped to click with the congressman, to find him as eager to support my personal development as I was eager to assist him—and that wasn't the direction this interview was going.

"Well, Neil, a few housekeeping items to discuss," Congressman Sibal said, looking at his watch. "My office is very crowded, but there's an annex office on the top floor of this building, which is where you'd be stationed."

I nodded my head, and he continued.

"As for chain of command, you would be reporting to my legislative assistant on a daily basis."

I nodded again.

"If this all sounds good to you, Neil, the job's yours."

I thanked Congressman Sibal, shook his hand good-bye, and assured him that I looked forward to seeing him in a few months. And then I walked quickly toward the office exit. Already I felt as if I'd imposed upon his morning schedule; I wanted to get out of his hair fast.

I returned to the seemingly endless hallways of the Cannon House Office Building and started making my way toward the main exit. Mission accomplished. Right? I'd secured my summer employment, and now I had the whole day ahead of me to play. I should have been ecstatic.

But I wasn't.

I just kept picturing myself slaving away in that secluded back office, as far from the action as a person could get, filing paperwork, cranking out cookie-cutter constituent letters using generic responses that had been prepared by others.

ONE HUNDRED DOORS

I'm going to be lost and forgotten back there, I thought. *I'll never get to see the congressman.* I certainly didn't have the feeling that someone would be keeping an eye out for me, making sure I had a great internship experience, that I actually learned something.

Maybe I'm setting my expectations too high, I reasoned. I mean, I *had* just gotten what I'd come down to D.C. to get: an internship with the congressman of my choice. And I had gotten it from my very first interview.

Yet it didn't feel good. It didn't feel right.

I had to think. I needed to find a place where I could sort this all out. I looked around—nothing. There was nowhere to sit, not even a bench, so I found my way to the cafeteria in the Longworth House Office Building, purchased a bottle of water and a chocolate chip cookie, and sat down to do some serious thinking.

I knew what I wanted out of an internship. I wanted to work on policy issues that were important. I wanted to have an impact even though I was a nineteen-year-old with no meaningful work experience. These things were more important to me than what a congressman's political philosophy was or which district he represented.

I decided to go for it. Then and there, just twenty minutes after a successful interview with Congressman Sibal, I decided to get what I *really* wanted out of an internship.

So I returned to the Cannon House Office Building, found my way to the first door on the first floor, and walked in. "Hi, I'm Neil Peterson," I said to the receptionist, "and I'm looking for a summer internship position. Is the congressman available?"

I didn't even know which congressman's office this was, or else I would have asked for him by name. Needless to say, I didn't get very far. The receptionist politely thanked me for coming in, told me that the congressman was in a meeting at the moment, and asked if I had a resume to leave behind, which I promptly handed her.

I returned to the hallway, walked to the next congressman's office, and went in. "Hi, I'm Neil Peterson," I said, smiling at the next receptionist. "I'm looking for a summer internship position and wonder if the congressman is available."

This time the receptionist asked, "Mr. Peterson, do you have an appointment with the congressman?"

Of course I didn't. So I stepped back into the hallway and walked to the next congressman's door. I did this for the rest of the afternoon, moving from one congressman's office to the next. Each response was different.

"Mr. Peterson, do you live in the district?"

"Mr. Peterson, I'm sorry. We've already filled all of our summer intern positions."

"Mr. Peterson, the congressman is currently in his home district. Would you like to make an appointment for when he returns next week?"

At the end of the workday, I headed back to where I was spending the night. But I returned the next day and once again walked down the halls of Congress, knocking on doors.

No luck.

I went back the following day and repeated the same thing.

I must have knocked on one hundred doors.

Around 11 a.m. on the third day of my hunt, I got a refreshingly different response. I said the usual, "Hi, I'm Neil Peterson. I'm looking for a summer internship position and wondered if the congressman is available."

"Could you wait here, Mr. Peterson?" the receptionist responded. "Let me check with the congressman to see if he's available."

Oh, my gosh! I thought. *You mean there's a chance I might see a congressman?*

I didn't know anything about him, except that he was from Florida and a Democrat. And his name was Charles E. Bennett.

The receptionist came out of the congressman's office. "The congressman will see you," she said. I couldn't believe it.

I walked into what seemed, to me, a very big office. The congressman was sitting behind a huge cherry desk. His gray hair was cropped short, with a part on the left, and he wore white-rimmed glasses. He was smooth-shaven and dressed in a simple but well-pressed suit.

*"If I can slay even one of those dragons—just one—
then I have done my job."
—Congressman Charles E. Bennett*

He struggled to get up, using a cane to stand. But he didn't move from behind the desk. I quickly walked up to the desk and leaned over to shake his hand. He was above average height, close to six feet. And he had a fun, wry smile.

"Please, sit down," he said, motioning to a chair. I took a seat opposite his desk, and he sat too, almost with as much effort as it had taken him to stand. He reached down to adjust something on his knee. I realized he wore a brace.

I scanned the room briefly, trying to take it all in. I couldn't get over the size of his office. About ten feet from his desk was a coffee table, flanked by a couch and two large armchairs. Then, in the far corner of the room, was another circular table surrounded by four captain's chairs. Bookcases overflowing with books covered the walls. Several books and what looked like manuscripts caught my eye because they were displayed so prominently. I squinted to see the titles, but all I could see was the author's name—"Charles E. Bennett."

"I understand that you're looking for a summer internship," Congressman Bennett said.

"Yes, sir."

"Well," he said, "tell me a little about yourself and your political beliefs."

I did, and he listened intently, still smiling. When I finished, he told me about himself.

"I've been in Congress for twenty-two years," he said. "I represent the Jacksonville, Florida, area. I am the third most senior member on the House Armed Services Committee. I served in World War II and contracted polio. As a result, I have a leg brace and have to use a cane to walk. But what I am most proud of is that I have the longest record in the House of Representatives for never having missed a vote. I haven't missed a vote in nineteen years."

I listened intently, but I couldn't help but focus my attention beyond him for just a few seconds. There was a huge window behind his desk, the only window in the office, and it framed a dramatic view of the domed Capitol building. It was breathtaking. I snuck a glance and then quickly returned to looking him straight in the eye.

"My political philosophy is very conservative," he said, "even though I am a Democrat. I get a check every month from the U.S. Treasury because I am a disabled American veteran...and every month I send that check back to the Treasury and instruct them to use it to reduce the size of the American debt."

"Really, sir? That's impressive."

He smiled. "So, what is it that you're looking for in an internship?"

I was so glad he'd asked. Thanks to my epiphany in the cafeteria, I knew exactly what I wanted.

"There are two things, sir," I responded. "One is to see everything that you, the congressman, do. And the second is to be involved in a policy issue where I can have some impact."

He considered my answer for what seemed like minutes but was probably just seconds.

"My administrative assistant, which is the top staff job in a congressman's office, is more conservative than I am," he responded. "I could use someone in my office who provides some balance. I could use someone who has a liberal philosophy, to provide another viewpoint as I face critical issues this summer."

This was heading in a very positive direction.

"How would this be…" he started, leaning in a bit as he prepared to outline his proposed working arrangement. I was on the edge of my chair.

"First," he said, "I will move a desk into my office for you, so you can literally see everything that I do. How would that be?"

This is amazing! my mind screamed. But I simply nodded my head in agreement.

"Second," he continued, "I'll put you in charge of the research that I need to do on the anti-poverty bill that President Lyndon Johnson is proposing and that will come to vote this summer. I haven't decided yet how I will vote on that, and you will be my key staff person on that policy issue. How would that be?"

"Mr. Congressman," I said, "that would be wonderful. Thank you so much." I stood up and leaned over the desk to shake his hand so that he wouldn't have to stand again. "We have a deal."

He smiled genuinely. I knew it was going to be a great summer. We spoke a few more minutes until I felt I should let him get back to work, and then I said good-bye.

As I walked out of his office, I had a huge smile on my face. I knew this was the right place for me. I didn't care that he was conservative and I was liberal. I didn't care that he was from Jacksonville, Florida, and I was from New Canaan, Connecticut. Those details didn't make any difference. What was important was that he was willing to open himself up and listen to me, a nineteen-year-old kid.

I walked down the hall, returned to Congressman Sibal's office, and told his legislative assistant I was very grateful for the internship offer but that I had decided to do something else for the summer.

✳ ✳ ✳

The payoff from those three days of knocking on Capitol Hill doors extended well beyond that summer's internship.

Congressman Bennett, or "Charlie," and I got along so well that he asked me to return the next summer, 1964, to help him with his campaign for reelection. He was very worried about his reelection because Barry Goldwater was running as the Republican presidential candidate, and Goldwater promised to pull to the polls a lot of conservative voters who, for the first time, might vote against Charlie. Plus, Charlie had, for the first time in twenty years, an opponent who was well financed.

So he sent me to Jacksonville as his deputy campaign manager—and he paid me! I loved it. In the end, Charlie's worries were unfounded, as he handily won the election with 72 percent of the vote in a district where Goldwater got just over 50 percent.

But the true payoff was simply getting to know Charlie. He was such a wonderful human being—so honest, so spiritual, so grounded in core values—and extremely hardworking and dedicated. He would come into the office at five o'clock each morning and personally dictate responses to each of his constituents' letters. No other congressman did this.

Charlie and I became very close, almost like father and son. He conveyed to me that he'd felt disappointments with his son—and the biggest disappointment in my life was my father. So in a way, we had a common bond. I guess we each filled a need for the other.

We ended up staying in touch well beyond the two summers I worked for him. With sadness, I learned of his passing away in 2003.

When I think of Charlie today, I remember his dedication, his hard work, his determination. And without fail, I always see in my mind a picture on his wall.

During my interview that spring, I had spotted a painting on the wall behind his desk, to the left of the window. From what I could tell, it was a picture of St. George, slaying the dragon.

"Is there any special meaning to that picture?" I had asked.

"Why, yes there is, Neil," he had answered. "The dragon represents all the things that frustrate and block the average person. If I can slay even one of those dragons—just one—then I have done my job."

This, I believe, is why we were kindred spirits.

Looking back, I am so glad I refused to settle for the first internship I was handed—and grateful that my hunt led me to Charlie's door. What I gained from my persistence paid off for a lifetime, as I learned from Charlie a lot about campaigning, the political process, and how to meet and greet voters—but even more importantly, the value of hard work, the importance of being absolutely honest, and the sheer joy of giving of yourself to help others.

ELEVEN

My Intellectual Autobiography

Believing in Oneself

James MacGregor Burns was one of the most well-known professors at Williams College during my four years of study there. A political science professor and head of the poli sci department, he was also a presidential biographer who won a Pulitzer Prize for his book *Roosevelt: Soldier of Freedom 1940-1945*. He has written more than two dozen books to date, including a biography in the mid '60s of then-new president John Fitzgerald Kennedy, to whom he was close in part because of his attendance as a delegate to at least four Democratic National Conventions, as well as his being a Democratic candidate for Congress. In recent years Burns has been a pioneer in the study of leadership and has written several authoritative works in that field.

As a poli sci major, I couldn't wait to take Professor Burns' senior honors class and sit under the tutelage of such a renowned and prolific man. I had taken courses with Professor Burns before—for example, his well-known American Political Parties course. And I'd even had the opportunity to work alongside him when I headed up Young Citizens for Johnson-Humphrey in northwestern Massachusetts in 1964. He sat as faculty advisor, and through that experience, we got to know each other reasonably well.

I was more than eager to be in a senior-level course with Professor Burns and benefit from a closer student-professor relationship. Class sizes at Williams were never large, but with only fifteen students enrolled in the senior honors course, the class would be entirely different from anything I'd experienced up to that point in my college career—more hands-on, more interactive, more intimate.

But even better than the small class size was the senior honors thesis we were expected to complete as part of the course. Many students cringed at the thought of tackling a one-hundred-plus-page senior-level paper, but I couldn't wait to get started. I welcomed the opportunity to apply the knowledge I'd gained during my preceding three years of study at Williams.

As Professor Burns handed out a syllabus on the first day of class, I wondered what burning issue of the day the thesis topic would have to address. Apartheid in South Africa? The effect of the war in Vietnam on America's domestic political agenda? How the Civil Rights struggle in America would be different in the future given the landmark legislation that was passed under President Johnson in the wake of Kennedy's death?

To my surprise—and everyone else's—the senior thesis was none of these. Instead, Professor Burns selected one much more personal: "Your Intellectual Autobiography." Our thesis was to communicate what we believed at the young age of twenty-one, why we held those beliefs, and how we'd developed them.

Wow!

I jumped into the assignment enthusiastically, attacking it with the same energy I bring to any project I set my mind to. I read, researched, and reflected. I interviewed my parents, my grandmothers, my girlfriend, my two best friends, and my college roommates. I self-administered several tests to get a better sense of myself, including Lane's ego strength scale, a conservatism-liberalism scale, the Rosenberg faith-in-people scale, an authoritarianism scale, a dominance scale, and the "M" measure, which tests the degree of attitudinal acceptance or rejection of minority groups.

Professor James MacGregor Burns was
"someone who believed in me"

I scoured previous school records and teacher comments for clues about how others viewed me and what they saw as my guiding beliefs.

I asked questions, questions, and more questions.

How had my parents' values and ideologies affected my own?

How had the environment of my hometown colored my belief system?

What role did our family history and economic status play in the development of my worldview?

How had my education molded me?

What impact did significant life experiences have on my beliefs?

I was so intent on my research that I didn't even go home for Thanksgiving. I labored on the thesis straight through the vacation, never leaving campus, thankful for the opportunity to get more work done without interruptions.

My hard work paid off. When I received the 125-page thesis back from Professor Burns, the title page had a big "A+" splashed across it in red ink. Next to the grade were these words from Professor Burns:

> *An impressive document that effectively combines both your personal and intellectual development. Candid in approach, steady in focus, deep-probing in analysis, this paper is one of the two or three best that I have had…*

Because of the thesis, five months later at commencement, I received the Arthur B. Graves Essay Prize, established by Graves in 1858 for the best essay prepared by a senior in political science.

It was rewarding. Thrilling. Invigorating. For a young man who had struggled his whole school career with a yet-to-be-diagnosed learning disability, the accolades were intoxicating.

Beyond that, the praise touched my heart and gave me a much-yearned-for comfort. It was as if all the pats on the back I'd craved over the years but had never received were finally being wrapped up and given to me all at once. Finally I was hearing the words, "Good job, son."

Years later, I understood more deeply what writing my thesis had given me. In 1987, five years before his death, Paul Ylvisaker gave a speech at the 1987 International Outward Bound Conference in Cooperstown, New York, that captured the essence of learning. Paul, who had served as Dean of the Harvard Graduate School of Education, Commissioner of Community Affairs for the State of New Jersey, and Director of National Affairs for the Ford Foundation, was my mentor and professor in graduate school. He also offered me my first full-time job after graduation.

"There is no learning without challenge and emotion," Paul said in that speech. "The things you learn the best…are emotional in character."

In writing my thesis, I came to realize that what made me *me* hadn't been gleaned from textbooks, lectures, or homework assignments. The essence of who I was—what I believed, what I valued, what made me tick—was, as Paul so poignantly captured in his speech many years later, the sum total of the emotion-filled experiences I'd had in life.

The father who wouldn't play ball with me.

The parents who were indifferent to my eighth-grade school election victory.

The high school headmaster who told my parents I was working "too hard" to compensate for my lack of intellect.

Paul had another insight that day that has stuck with me. "What makes a difference?" he asked. "Why did you succeed, and why do your brothers sometimes fail?"

Paul, answering his own question, responded, "I met a caring person. Someone who believed in me—a mother, a teacher, a taxi cab driver, a neighbor. Somebody took an interest in and treated me as a worthy human being."

Professor Burns was one of these caring persons about whom Paul spoke—"someone who believed in me." And there had been others, too. My classical Greek teacher. My high school hockey coach. The congressman under whom I'd interned the previous summer. My college hockey coach. As I wrote my paper, I realized that these individuals had largely shaped who I was, what I believed, and why I believed as I did. And because these individuals believed in me, I was able to excel, to push beyond the expected, and to achieve something great.

They reaffirmed to me the value of a good mentor, for it was only because of them that I was able to persevere.

TWELVE
Cambridge City Manager

Holding to High Standards

I knew instantly that I had made the right decision.

❋ ❋ ❋

In 1972, at twenty-eight years of age, I wanted to get back into what I called the real world. I had spent the last three years working for Booz, Allen & Hamilton, providing management consulting for clients all over the United States as well as in Mexico and Panama. The exposure I received at Booz Allen was extensive, but more important, I learned an approach to problem solving that I will be able to use for the rest of my life no matter what I am doing or where I am located.

Nevertheless, I chafed in the role of a consultant, advising others who would put my suggestions into effect. I yearned to get back to the role of decision maker, making the call and taking the responsibility for my actions. My previous job as city administrator of New Brunswick, New Jersey, was such a job. It had been stressful but packed with decisions that affected people on a day-to-day basis. I missed the action.

So after three years at Booz Allen, I began to look around for an opportunity to get back into a position that excited me.

I heard that there was an opening for the city manager of Cambridge, Massachusetts.

Cambridge, with a population of just over a hundred thousand residents, was one of the biggest cities in America to have a city manager form of government and was viewed within the city management profession as one of its premier positions. Apart from that, it had its share of challenges. Home of Harvard University and Massachusetts Institute of Technology (MIT), Cambridge had the reputation of being one of the most liberal cities in the country. Its politicians were dealing with issues that other cities' officials would not even dream of getting involved in.

Cambridge's city council was viewed as very progressive and, to some, even radical. It had on it Sandra Graham, a very aggressive, young black woman, a welfare mother, who made national news on June 11, 1970, by leading a low-income housing sit-in and demonstration that disrupted Harvard University's commencement exercises.

Before I applied for the position, I did a little homework. I discovered that, out of the several hundred candidates, two of the most experienced and well regarded city managers in the country were applying for the position. One was city manager of Kansas City, Missouri, and the other of Schenectady, New York.

An acquaintance of mine, Steve Farber, who had gone to the Woodrow Wilson School at Princeton with me, was an assistant to the then president of Harvard University, Derek Bok. I gave Steve a call and asked him what he knew about the city manager opening, the lay of the land, and whether it was already wired for someone. He said he did not know himself but he would make some inquiries. He called back and said that it was truly an open process but that some heavyweights were applying.

So, I said to myself, *Why not apply? If nothing else, it will be good experience. And I have nothing to lose. Why not?*

Somehow in the process, I was selected as one of four finalists. My guess is that Steve and Harvard used their influence at least to get me in the game. But I really do not know how this occurred.

In typical Cambridge fashion, the city council decided to involve the public in its deliberations on who the next city manager of Cambridge would be. One newspaper called it "an orgy of citizen participation." The council set up a process which set aside a Saturday where all four finalists would come to Cambridge and be interviewed by citizens. Hundreds of citizens were broken into four groups of fifty to seventy each, which then met with, heard from, and interviewed each of the candidates. These interview sessions lasted about ninety minutes each.

At the end of the day, each group of citizens came together to give its recommendations to the city council so that the council members could take the citizens' input into account as they made the final decision on which candidate to offer the job to. This involvement and process was, and to this day still is, highly unusual. I have never heard of a city doing something like this.

So I hopped a flight from New Jersey, where I was living at the time, to Boston and anxiously prepared for the day of interviewing by the public.

I knew that I had no business being considered in the same breath with at least two of the other three candidates. They were seasoned city managers with years of experience under their belts. And both were well regarded in the profession.

In contrast, I was not even thirty years old. I had been a city administrator for only two years. And my city of New Brunswick, New Jersey, had a population barely half that of Cambridge's and significantly less than those of my known competitors.

This wasn't a fair fight. It wasn't even a close call.

Knowing all of this, I was able to be very relaxed about what would surely be an unusual day of give-and-take, questioning, and interviewing. I knew I had nothing to lose. So I could relax and be myself and enjoy the experience.

And I did. I got into it. I loved it. I was engaged.

For example, they asked me my thoughts about the city-sponsored day-care program, the only city in the nation at that time to have such a program. I told them that I was all for it and that the challenge for the city would be to find a way to make the program sustainable over time because the need was so far greater than the resources available.

At the end of the day, the four groups of citizens gave their recommendations to the city council, and to my shock, they all recommended me. Yes, me.

Holy cow!!!! I'd wowed them. I'd connected with them. I'd had a love-in.

Local papers called the process "pretty revealing," commenting that "Peterson had an extraordinarily candid manner." Adding that I had a "breadth of appeal," the paper cited that I was the choice of both the Cambridge police representative and the Cambridge Tenants' Organizing Committee representative.

The city council was shocked. While the position may not have been wired in advance, the council had a sense of who it was going to pick, and I was definitely not that person. This result created a real stir. And a problem.

The members debated for days on what to do. The individual on the council who became my champion turned out to be Sandra Graham, the most radical member of the council. She said, "The people have spoken. We, the city council, asked for their input. They gave it to us. We need to honor it."

The days turned into weeks. No decision came from the city council until one day I got a call from the president of the city council, telling me that I had been chosen to be the next city manager of Cambridge, Massachusetts.

I was ecstatic. I *really* wanted this position. This was such a feather in my cap. It was a prestigious spot, significant in the profession, and cutting edge in terms of dealing with the problems of urban America.

But the vote on the council had been 5 to 4.

Such lack of unanimity—or the failure to garner at least two-thirds support—is never a good sign and a major warning signal for an incoming city manager. But given my age and the "nothing to lose" approach, I was willing to take the position even on a 5 to 4 vote.

The president of the council asked me to fly up to Boston the next day to make the announcement publicly in front of all of the media. I said sure, I would be there.

Later on that day, I received phone calls from individual council members congratulating me. One such call was from one of the council members who had voted for me. He asked if I could stop by his Boston office on the way to the press conference the next day. I said sure.

The next day I arrived in Boston as scheduled, hailing a taxi to take me to the council office.

In his quarters, he congratulated me again. He said that he wanted to talk to me about some issues privately that were very important to him. I said, "Great. I want to hear what those are. I'll try to be as responsive as I can."

He began by saying, "I'm very concerned about the representation of blacks on the city staff." The councilman is black; he was impeccably dressed in his suit and tie.

He added, "I want to make sure that blacks are adequately represented on the city staff—both in terms of numbers and in what positions they hold."

I responded quickly, "I appreciate your position completely, and I agree with the philosophy that you are espousing. I had the very same goal when I was city administrator in New Brunswick, and my track record speaks for itself. I will do everything I can to make sure that what you are asking for happens."

Then he pulled out a piece of folded white paper from the breast pocket of his suit jacket. He began to read me the names of individuals that he wanted to have jobs at city hall.

I immediately responded, "My policy will be what it was in New Brunswick—namely, that for any individuals referred to me by a council member, not only will they be given the opportunity to apply for positions and go through the process like everybody else, but in addition, I will personally sit down and meet with the individuals that any councilmember forwards to me."

He looked at me. No, he stared at me. And he said, "Neil, I don't believe you understand me. I want these individuals to get jobs in city hall." And he handed me the white paper with the list of individuals on it.

I repeated to him what I had said earlier, emphasizing that I would personally interview anybody he would refer for a job. But I added that, beyond that, the individual would be chosen based upon merit as the best person for the job.

He turned and walked away and took off his suit jacket. He stood at the window of his office, looking out on the City of Boston. He began to recount for me his family history. Then he turned toward me again and said, "Neil, you know that I'm the fifth vote. If I don't vote for you, you don't get the job. You know that, right?"

I looked him square in the eyes. I knew exactly what he was saying. I was very aware of what he was demanding from me. And I knew exactly the implications of what I was saying in return.

"I don't operate that way. I will agree to your policy objective wholeheartedly. I will bend over backward to personally see, interview, and acknowledge your referrals for jobs. But I will not agree to hire Sam or Suzie or Jim because you said so or because you could fire me tomorrow. The hiring and firing decisions of city staff will be made by me and my staff alone, without undue or inappropriate influence from individual council members."

I got up from my chair, turned, and walked out the door. I took the elevator down the many stories, hailed a taxi, and said to the driver, "Take me to the airport."

The press conference never happened. Weeks later the city council appointed someone else to lead the city for the future.

And I was looking for another job.

And, oh, had I wanted that job. I had so yearned for it. I was willing to do almost anything to get it. But what I found out, to my pleasant surprise, was that I was not willing to compromise my values and my being. I was not willing to do quite *anything* to get that plum position.

"Neil, you know that I'm the fifth vote?"

I realized that, had I taken the job, I would have carried in my heart the wrong I'd done for years to come—and it would have eaten at me. I wouldn't have been able to live with it.

I learned more about myself in not getting that job than I have in working at many of the jobs I have taken since then. I experienced more growth and maturity in not getting that job than I have acquired in years of working at others. It was a defining moment in my life.

My resume makes no mention of Cambridge city manager. And yet, my letting this job slip from my fingers at the very moment I knew it could have been mine belongs at the top of those experiences crucial to my job performance.

Sometimes you learn more from what you don't do than from what you do do.

THIRTEEN
Long-Board Shuffleboard

Enjoying the Game

Who would have thought that a little-known sport would lead to a great story?

But it did.

The setting was Olympia, the capital of the State of Washington. The year was 1977.

I was a relatively young, energetic thirty-year-old state worker for the Department of Social and Health Services (DSHS), and I'd just moved my family and myself out from Princeton, New Jersey. As a newcomer to the Olympia area, I wanted to explore and experience the ways of the Pacific Northwest as much as possible.

This included going to my first logging festival in Shelton, Washington. I will never forget that experience, not because of the lumberjack competitions but because of the behavior of the spectators. Prior to walking with my wife and two kids into the quasi-stadium where the festival was being held, I carefully put my six-pack of beer in a brown paper bag so that nobody would notice I was carrying it in. After finding seats in the stands for all of us, I broke out a beer, carefully wrapping it in a brown bag, again so nobody would notice what I was really doing.

As we waited for the festival to begin, with its logrolling, wood-chopping, tree-climbing, and other events, I noticed other people walking in, blantantly carrying whole cases of beer under their arms. And they didn't have paper bags around them. They were walking in with beer, in broad daylight for all to see. *Holy cow*, I thought to myself. *Wow*. And then suddenly it dawned on me that I was attending a logging festival in the Northwest. *Get with it, Neil*, I thought to myself. *Of course, beer is allowed.* I knew then that my experience in Washington was going to be a whole lot different from any I'd had on the East Coast.

In the mid-seventies, Olympia, Washington, was an exciting place to work because of the leadership of key politicians—then third-term Governor Dan Evans, Charlie Morris at DSHS, and John Bagnariol and others in the legislature.

A few of us self-described "young hot-shots" found out that the best luncheon sandwiches in town were served at a dive tavern called the Brotherhood. This was the kind of place that opened at 6 a.m. in order to accommodate the loggers and others either just coming off work or just going to work. Beer at 6 a.m.! Yes, Washington was sure different.

The Brotherhood was a man's bar with stiff drinks, crazy paintings, and a great jukebox. It attracted a grizzled older crowd, but a few of us would, nonetheless, go down to the tavern a few times a week for lunch. It was quite a sight, I'm sure, to see us state employees with our suit pants, collared shirts, and ties, sitting right next to the hardcore patrons in their flannel shirts, rugged jeans, and steel-toe boots. But the sandwiches were great and continued to draw us week after week.

Plus we had entertainment. In the back of the tavern was a long-board shuffleboard, the first I had ever seen. Twenty-two feet long, thirty-two inches wide, and thirty-one inches tall…a thick hardwood butcher-block bed made of maple, with a smooth, glossy, lacquer finish, a perfect home for eight fast-shooting, roller-bearing pucks.

Long-board shuffleboard has been around in one form or another for centuries

The sport has been around in one form or another for centuries. In his plays, William Shakespeare referred to "shovelboard," an ancestor to today's long-board shuffleboard. The goal of the sport—and it *is* a sport in Olympia, not just a game—is to get the puck as close to the end of the board as possible without going off the end of the board. You get a point for every puck of yours that is closer to the end than any of your competitor's. As in curling, the player controls the puck for only a short time, pushing it toward the far end. The skill lies in judging the distance and speed correctly and carefully positioning the puck down the long board. Scoring for the game is similar to bocce and curling.

It's a team sport. You shoot against your competitor at your end, and then your partner shoots against your competitor's partner at the other end of the table. The first team to get 21 points wins the game.

Shuffleboard's a big deal in Washington. In 2006 there were fourteen shuffleboard tournaments in Washington state alone. The sport is popular elsewhere as well. Eighteen states, plus Canada, have official shuffleboard leagues.

During our lunches, my fellow state workers and I would watch the old-timers play the game. We were impressed by how much talent, skill, and strategy were required.

One day at lunch the bartender-cook-owner came to our table and asked if any of us wanted to play shuffleboard that night on the Brotherhood Shuffleboard Team in the Olympia Shuffleboard League. They were one person short that day, and unless one of us would play, they would have to forfeit the game.

In a moment of weakness, and with the motive of wanting to experience as much as possible of the Northwest culture, I said I would do it. He gave me directions to a tavern on the outskirts of town. It was an away game!

What an experience. That tavern was packed. All to watch the match.

These guys were pros. Our old-timers on the Brotherhood Shuffleboard Team were good, but these guys on the other team were *awesome*. Unbelievable. And of course I was terrible, having never shot a shuffleboard puck in my life. I had shot a lot of hockey pucks, but obviously that skill was not transferable to shuffleboard; it did me absolutely no good.

Aside from showing up so that our team didn't have to default, I ended up not helping our team one bit. In fact, we got creamed. The other team massacred us. It was a total blowout.

The game took more than three hours to play. It seemed as if everyone was drinking beer and smoking the entire time. By the time the match was over, I was beat. The next morning I struggled to drag myself to work.

The next day, my coworkers and I had our usual sandwiches for lunch at the Brotherhood. As we were eating, the bartender-cook-owner came over and announced that the old-timers had all quit the team in disgust.

"You're the captain," he said to me. "Get yourself a team."

Needless to say, I was dumbfounded, but that lasted only a second or two. I quickly composed myself, smiled, and turned to my lunch buddies. "You're playing," I said to each of them. They were my first recruits as I started the process of putting together a team. By the time I was done, I had recruited quite a group of players, including…

- Ken Miller, who worked for me at DSHS. Ken had attended the same graduate school as I had, the Woodrow Wilson School of Public and International Affairs at Princeton University.

- Bob Lewis, who worked for me at DSHS.

- Gene Schlatter, who at the time was the chief staff person for the House Ways and Means Committee of the Washington State Legislature.

- John Bagnariol (or "Baggy," as we called him), who was the powerful chairman of the House Ways and Means Committee. Later, in 1980, he was indicted for gambling-related racketeering in a joint FBI-state police operation called Gamscam, for which he was convicted and served ten years in federal prison.

- Pat Gallagher, who was a lobbyist at the time. He also was indicted and convicted in Gamscam of racketeering in a plot to legalize slot machines and casino gambling in exchange for a cut of the profits.

- Orin Smith, who was the Budget Director for the State, the head of the Office of Fiscal Management, the governor's key appointment. He later became the CEO of Starbucks Coffee.

- Yours truly, who at the time was the head of the Office of Management and Budget in the Department of Social and Health Services.

Our team was made up entirely of state employees, in stark contrast to the "down-home" composition of the other teams. We stood out for another, more important reason, as well. Our team was made up, 100 percent, of individuals who had no experience—absolutely none—in playing shuffleboard. But inexperience never held me back, nor did it my compatriots. After all, our purpose was to have fun. And that we did. The one part of the game that we were particularly good at was drinking beer. We could hold our own in that regard.

We played at least one match a week, sometimes two. The season lasted an unbelievable forty weeks—almost ten months! This was a sport that you had to be in shape for.

Even with so many games—and the obligatory late-night drinking—we managed to drag ourselves into work the next day after every match. Nonetheless, the hours of playing, drinking, and pressure took their toll on us. I could see it in the faces of the other players when they would report to work the next morning at 8 a.m. We were all beat.

We played every match. And we lost every match we played. Our track record was embarrassing, but we had a blast.

In a strange way, the "locals" who populated all of the other eleven teams in the league liked us. They reacted well to us, even though we were wearing suits and ties. I believe it was because we didn't fit their image of state workers—namely, stuffy, snooty, not willing to mingle with the local folk, not willing to get their hands dirty. In contrast, we

Third place, B Division, Olympia Shuffleboard League, 1977

were willing to engage with them, to have some fun, to drink lots of beer. And I think they admired our fortitude, our ability to smile (I know the beer helped here) while we were mercilessly beaten week in and week out.

Thankfully, the season was divided into two halves. At the end of the first half of the season, the best six teams were placed in the "A" division, and the worst six teams were placed in the "B" division. And then, for the second half of the season, we started over with a clean slate.

The fresh start gave us a chance to improve our record. And with all of the practice we had gotten from our losses during the first half of the season, we actually got better during the second half. Believe it or not. We learned some of the techniques that were necessary to be successful at shuffleboard. These included—to name just a few—using both hands, "side wheeling," the use of "English," blocking your own pucks, and attacking your opponent's pucks.

As the second half of the season unfolded, an amazing thing happened. We began to win. We actually posted some victories! We were ecstatic. And we were beginning to take it pretty seriously.

At the end of the season, the league had a big party at the local volunteer firehouse. The place was packed. They handed out awards, and miraculously, we received one. Not just any award, but the biggest award I have ever received playing any sport in my entire life. The team trophy had to be three feet tall. And the individual trophies that were handed out to each of the team members were big, too, almost two feet tall apiece.

And that award we received was for coming in third in the B division of the Olympia Shuffleboard League in 1977. Quite an achievement for rookies!

Winning that trophy was one of the goofiest and yet most rewarding moments of my life. Never in a million years would I have guessed I would compete in a long-board shuffleboard tournament, and yet here we were, winning a trophy. To this day, my award sits right in the middle of the shelf in my studio that I've set aside for displaying various awards and honors.

FOURTEEN
Riding the Buses

Going the Extra Mile(s)

As I left Olympia, my head was throbbing. I felt uneasy, nervous, lacking in confidence.

I was on my way to interview with a special executive search committee for the post of executive director of Seattle Metro. Metro, as it was known to the locals, had probably the best reputation of any public agency in Washington State, perhaps even in the country. It was an outstanding organization.

Founded in 1958 under the leadership of Jim Ellis, it was the brainchild of citizens who were fed up with pollution in Lake Washington—so bad at the time that swimming was actually banned. The citizens went to the state legislature and got legislation passed that permitted the formation of a new regional government to deal with problems such as water quality, subject to a vote by the people affected. The citizens put the issue to the voters, and the voters responded by creating Metro. In a great success story, Lake Washington was cleaned up. Metro did its job.

Basking in this triumph, Metro then asked voters whether to rescue the failing, almost bankrupt private mass transportation companies and create a public mass transportation system for the region. Again the voters said yes. Since that time in the early '70s, Metro has grown to be perhaps the best large public transportation system in the country, known for its high-quality staff, its goal orientation, and its regional focus.

It rained as I drove the sixty miles from Olympia to Seattle to interview for the position. Another rainy Washington day. Cool with a chill in the air. Low clouds formed a tent above, as if the sky had moved closer to the earth. It fit my mood. I hoped for sun tomorrow, the day of the interview—or at least for a break in the rain—to lift my spirits and give me the extra mental "push" I needed.

I was nervous for several reasons—and justifiably so. First, I had no background or experience in either transportation or water quality. I had spent the last four years running programs at the Department of Social and Health Services (DSHS)—programs such as welfare, social services, foster care, juvenile rehabilitation, and support organizations to address alcoholism, drug abuse, aging, and mental health. It was interesting work, but it had no real connection to transportation or water quality.

My trepidation also stemmed from the fact that Metro's board of directors comprised some of the most important political and civic figures in Seattle.

John Spellman, executive of King County, who would later become governor.

Wes Uhlman, mayor of the City of Seattle.

Carey Donworth, a businessman who knew everybody in town and had served more than twenty years as chairman of the Metro council.

Jim Ellis, lawyer, the most admired civic leader in Seattle, and father of Metro.

The list went on. These were the heavyweights of Seattle's public and civic life. I didn't know any of them, except by reputation. And I was intimidated. Even though I had a very responsible state government job in Olympia, I was only thirty-three years old at the time, and my contacts were primarily in the state capital, not in Seattle, the state's largest city.

Welcome aboard

Finally, I was shaken by the fact that my competition was Joe Miller, city manager of Bellevue, Washington. Joe had a well-deserved reputation for being an outstanding city manager—a reputation that extended well beyond the borders of the state of Washington.

I had started my career in the public sector as city manager of New Brunswick, New Jersey, and as a result, had a good understanding of the talents required to be a good city manager. I also had occasion to know who were the most celebrated managers in the country, and Joe Miller was one of them. He was sixteen years my senior, so he had age, experience, and reputation over me. And as city manager of the second largest city in the Seattle metropolitan area, he knew the region intimately.

I knew I was the underdog, and the tension I felt in facing such odds tightened around me as I made the drive north. After an hour of careful, strained driving on Interstate 5, I arrived in Seattle. I pulled my VW van into the Butler parking garage on Yesler Street.

I really wanted the job. I was ready to move on and up from my position at DSHS, and the opening for executive director of Metro fit the bill perfectly. I was determined to get it. But I knew I had to do something that would set me apart from the others—and give me an edge. I had a plan.

I walked a half block to the nearest Metro bus stop on Second Avenue. An elderly woman and a man with a cane were there, waiting for the bus. No overhead shelter. No bench to sit on. Just a street sign saying Metro Bus Stop. I joined them.

Yogi Berra supposedly once said, "You can observe a lot just by watching." That was my goal—to observe (and more important, to learn) as much as I could about Metro, just by watching.

Some learn auditorially, some visually. I learn best kinesthetically. It's important for me not only to see and hear about something but also actually to experience it—which was why I was going to ride the buses.

All day long.

The bus pulled up. I followed the other passengers up the steps and onto the bus. "Hi," I said with a nod to the driver.

"Welcome aboard!" he returned with a smile.

I took the seat closest to him, at the front right-hand side of the bus. I wanted to understand his world—to see everything he did, what pressures and challenges he faced.

I was amazed. I never had given much thought to what a bus driver's job entailed. Based on my observations, it was a great deal.

The first discovery that hit me was the awesome skill required to drive a forty-five-foot-long bus. Weaving in and out of traffic. Starting and stopping the great, bulky vehicle. Pulling in and out of stops. Putting up with the inevitable bad drivers and jaywalkers. Simply knowing which of the many buttons and gadgets on the console to press.

The second insight that struck me was the major responsibility involved in driving a bus. Not only are bus drivers responsible for a six-hundred-thousand-dollar vehicle, but they're also accountable for the lives of forty-some passengers on their bus at any one time. The young child going to school. The single parent trying to get to work. The businessman on his way to a meeting. The elderly man on his way to the library. The woman with a disability on her way home.

But the most amazing revelation for me was that the driver had to be an incredible personality—part salesperson, part social worker, part host. The driver had to be able to interact and deal with each customer. The many and varied situations the driver might face was mind-boggling.

Wow, I was impressed. I had no idea how challenging it was to be a bus driver.

I rode that bus for a good hour and then hopped on another. And then another. And another. I spent the entire day riding buses in the Seattle area, and I sat next to the driver on every single one, talking to each of them.

I asked them what they liked most about their jobs and what they liked the least. Why had they decided to become Metro bus drivers? What had been their careers before this job? What had their education been? I was amazed at how well educated most of the drivers were. Many had college degrees.

"Why this job?" I asked. "What is it about this job that really captures you?"

"It's the challenge," one driver responded. "Every single day is different. Every day has a new challenge. I love the contact with my riders."

The other thing that I couldn't help but notice was the interaction between the driver and the riders. It was close and warm. In fact, some of the passengers told me that they "loved" their driver. It wasn't just a ride on a bus. Their friendship with their driver was a big part of the experience for them, and vice versa for the driver.

I also asked the drivers about Metro. What was it like working for Metro? What did they think about its leadership? What did they see as the biggest issues facing Metro? What would they do differently if they were in charge?

The drivers were very open and forthcoming, very willing to talk. I think they knew that I had a genuine interest in them and their situation, and this encouraged them to open up and respond to my questions.

When the day was done, these bus drivers had given me a view of Metro from the ground floor, not the executive suite. It was precisely what I'd wanted.

The next morning I woke up at 6 a.m. in my hotel. I showered, shaved, and put on my suit and tie then ran out the front door and found the nearest bus stop. I was determined to get as much experience riding buses as I could before the interview later that morning.

I was still nervous about my interview but no longer anxious. I had prepared well for the meeting, and I knew I had nothing to fear. Instead, I felt keyed up, excited. I looked forward with pleasure to handling my interviewers' questions, even feeling a bit of a thrill at the anticipation of our upcoming exchange. After spending an entire day and a couple of hours that morning riding buses, I now had a good, hands-on feel for the operation of the public transportation responsibilities of Metro.

I was excited, because the people I had talked to were excited. I was ready.

"Your riders are my clients."

The most difficult question I had to answer during the interview was asked by County Executive John Spellman.

"Neil," he asked, "what background, training, or experience do you have in either public transportation or water quality?"

My answer was direct.

"Mr. Spellman," I responded, "I have no background, training, or experience in either public transportation or water quality."

The room got very quiet.

I moved slightly to the edge of my chair and continued.

"I spent yesterday riding your buses," I said. "I wanted to get an understanding, a feel, for what kind of service Metro is providing. I wanted to talk to the Metro drivers, the employees, who are the principal point of contact with your customers, the riding public. And I wanted to talk to the passengers about your service. So I rode buses all day long.

"What I learned from that experience is that your riders are my clients. Almost everyone who got on a Metro bus was either a young person, a single mom on welfare, an elderly person, a person who has a disability, individuals who may have mental health issues, or juveniles who may have been in trouble with the authorities. These people are my clients at DSHS. I've spent the last four years serving them."

My day riding the buses paid off. The search committee offered me the job, and I accepted it instantly.

My first few days on the job, I did the same thing I'd done the day before my interview—I made it my mission to get to know the drivers, the people on the front lines of the Metro organization. I met them at 4:30 each morning, to shake their hands before they boarded their buses and headed out to start their days. My goal was to show them my support, how much I appreciated their hard work and dedication. But even more importantly, I wanted to show them that I knew I still had a lot to learn—and that I was going to need their help in learning it.

I spent the next six years as CEO of Metro, the best job I ever had.

FIFTEEN
Not Alone on Christmas Day

Giving to Get

For three years after my divorce from my first wife, Ellen, I was alone on the important holidays. Thanksgiving and Christmas are days for families to gather and share. I was alone. All alone. As lonely as I felt, I knew the only one who could change the situation was Neil Peterson. I had to do something to keep from feeling sorry for myself and becoming depressed.

For Thanksgiving Day, I figured out that giving my time to others would not only help those in need but also help me step out of my own loneliness. So each year I helped serve Thanksgiving dinners to the homeless at the Union Gospel Mission in downtown Seattle. I felt great: I wasn't alone, and I was giving to others. As they say…it is more blessed to give than to receive.

For Christmas day, however, I decided to do something else.

My job at the time was running the Municipality of Metropolitan Seattle or, as most people called it, Metro. An independent regional government responsible for public transportation and water quality throughout the Seattle metropolitan area, Metro served almost three million people.

I had 3,500 employees working for me. Every holiday—and especially on Christmas day—we had just a skeleton staff in place to drive the buses, service the bus maintenance facilities, man the sewage treatment plants, and work the sewage pumping stations. I am sure that those employees, regardless of their religious practices, would have preferred to be with their families, enjoying a day off with the rest of the country, rather than to be stuck at work. I appreciated what they were doing and intended to let them know that.

So for three years, I got up very early on Christmas day and drove to each sewage treatment plant and each transit bus base to shake the hands of every staff person I could find who was working that day. I took all day.

The employees couldn't believe what I was doing—but they loved it. Somebody remembered them! Somebody thanked them for their sacrifice! And that somebody was the "big boss."

I loved it, too. It made me feel great because I knew my efforts made a difference to those employees. My simple handshake and few words sent a deeper message to them as well, and that message was, "You aren't alone, and your service is appreciated—especially on this holiday."

Surprisingly, by delivering this message to others, I discovered that I received the same in return.

"The more he gives to others, the more he possesses of his own" (Lao-tzu).

The loneliness I had felt had been just an illusion. Only by reaching out to others and giving what I thought I had lacked—a sense of connection, caring, and comfort—did I find those things within. By giving to others, I found a way of healing, of restoring what I thought I had lost.

That year, I discovered the true spirit of Christmas.

Thanksgiving dinner

SIXTEEN

Outward Bound

Confronting Fear

Only a handful of waterways in the United States bear the title "Wild and Scenic River." These rivers have been designated as "wilderness" through an act of Congress because of their outstanding natural qualities and scenic beauty. The Rogue River in Oregon, whose eighty-four mile "wilderness" section flows from Crater Lake to the Pacific Ocean, is one such protected river, beloved for its beauty, wildlife, and incredible rapids. I ran those rapids. In 1981, I joined an Outward Bound white-water rafting trip.

Outward Bound is a nonprofit organization that "changes lives, builds teams, and transforms schools." Through more hands-on, adventure-oriented activities than traditional classroom teaching, Outward Bound challenges individuals to reach their full potential—physically, mentally, emotionally, and spiritually.

I have always had a tremendous respect for Outward Bound. The organization emphasizes physical challenge as "an instrument for training the will to strive for mastery." And works with the underlying belief that an individual defines his or her reality through the "insistent use of action, as opposed to mind."

My first boss after graduate school, Greg Farrell, has since spent years with Outward Bound as the president and CEO of Expeditionary Learning Outward Bound, an urban education initiative that applies the methodology of the wilderness courses to more than two hundred elementary and secondary schools. These schools teach writing, reading, and math, but they do it in a way that incorporates experience, fieldwork, adventure, and service. The result? Self-confident children who internalize what they've learned.

I was invited on the trip on the Rogue River because Outward Bound was trying to recruit me to serve on its Northwest Advisory Board. I asked a friend, Bob Lewis, to come along with me. Originally from Chappaqua, New York, Bob had worked with me in state government in Olympia, Washington, and at Metro in Seattle. More important, Bob was my tennis buddy, my trout-fishing buddy, and my long-board shuffleboard buddy—in short, one of my best friends.

Bob and I were so excited about the rafting trip that we talked about it the entire seven-hour drive there. The allure of a grand adventure in tackling the white-water sections of the river thrilled us. We thought we might even be able to fit some fishing in during the evenings, but our major hope was to experience some serious and adventuresome white-water rafting.

The first full day of the rafting trip was spent reviewing safe rafting practices. With rapids ranging up to class IV intensity, the Rogue River was no walk in the park—or paddle on the pond. So the leaders spent a good chunk of time going through various safety drills with our group of about twelve people.

One such practice was the man-overboard drill, designed to teach us how to survive if we ever were to fall out of the raft—how to handle the river's current and speed as we were swept downstream out of reach of the raft, how to stay afloat, and how to avoid the huge boulders in the river that made up the rapids.

What we learned was that, first and foremost, we had to wear life-jackets and helmets at all times. Second, the goal was to float down the river feet first, lying on our backs. This would allow our feet to touch any rocks in the river first, thereby protecting our heads. Third, we were to put our arms out to the side as we floated, for balance and for steering.

After they'd illustrated how to float down the river safely, the trip leaders had us all paddle our rafts ashore at a particular bend in the river. They wanted us to put into practice what they'd taught us—to float down the river going through a set of rapids, lying on our backs, feet first, to get a first-hand feel for what they had been telling us. A real-life drill.

Great, I said to myself.

We all got out of our rafts and followed the leaders to a rocky promontory, where we scoped out the river and the rapids that we would be floating down.

Whoa! The rapids were huge, angry, churning. My palms started to sweat. My stomach moved halfway to my throat. *Are they for real? They really want us to ride down these rapids?*

After a few moments at the lookout point, we followed the Outward Bound leaders to the launch point, a short walking distance away, where we would each enter the river for our man-overboard drill. The leaders would then take our rafts and paddle them downstream, so that they'd be there to meet us at the end of the drill.

To my surprise, a woman I had assumed to be the least athletic, the least adventurous, offered to be the first one down the river. She was older, maybe in her late sixties, and she walked carefully, gingerly, her eyes glued to the ground with each step, a walking stick in her hand. Yet here she was, volunteering to go first. I couldn't believe it. She hopped right into the river and headed downstream without any visible trepidation.

A small group of us ran back to the rocky point to watch her navigate the huge rapids. Oh boy, did she ever have a ride. The waves looked to be at least eight feet tall, and she went up and over each one of them, keeping her man-overboard position the entire time. Finally, at the end of the rapids, where the water was calmer, she swam to shore, where an OB leader was waiting for her.

Pretty impressive, I said to myself.

Next was Jim Crutcher, a man in his late fifties and CEO of a construction company in Seattle. Then Jim's wife. Then Bob went down the river. One after another, each member of our group went down the river as I watched from shore.

Finally everyone had gone but me. There I was, all alone on shore. And scared to death.

I was shocked by my reaction. I had always thought of myself as a risk-taker, always willing to try something new. In fact, I constantly look for challenges, just so I can conquer them. But here I was, paralyzed with fear at the thought of traveling down that river.

I remained on the shore for a good five minutes, trying to summon enough courage to take the plunge. After pacing for a bit, trying to keep myself warm and to get my brain going, I finally took refuge on a rock. I sat there awhile, trying to get a hold of myself. I was so glad the rest of the group couldn't see me from their spot downstream. I didn't want them to see my hesitation.

Finally my fear of humiliation overcame my fear of the water. *What if you get stuck here?* I asked myself. *Do you really want to suffer that embarrassment? How would that look to the others in the group?*

I couldn't sit there any longer, I realized. The more I procrastinated, the harder it would be to make the trip downstream. Nervous but determined, I waded into the river. The water was jarringly cold. I began my float.

Here I go, I said to myself. *You can do it, Neil. You can do it.*

I put my feet out in front of me, my arms out to the side, spread-eagled. The river's current took over, propelling me downstream with increasing force. I could turn slightly by moving my arms, but not much.

Even though I was on my back, I could see the oncoming rapids as they swelled up in front of me. They were huge.

I couldn't see them, but I knew that there were rocks underneath the river's surface causing the angry waves. With each passing second, the sound of the water and the rapids grew in volume and intensity. What started as a strong but bearable "whooshing" transformed into

White-water rafting

thunderous "booms" the further I moved downstream. My float speed continued to increase as I approached the throat of the rapids.

Down the throat I went, into the trough of the rapid. Right in front of me was a mountain of water, three stories tall it seemed. I was certain the angry wave was going to fall on top of me, sucking me under and tumbling me about in its waters. *Will there be enough momentum to get me up and over the first rapid and onto the second one?* I asked myself. I closed my eyes, took a deep breath. *Bam!* Smack into the wall of water I went.

I opened my eyes. I hadn't been sucked under! Instead, the waters had carried me up and over the first rapid. I wanted to shout for joy, but there wasn't time. The next wall of water was seconds away, ready to decimate me if I didn't focus. I funneled all my energy toward keeping my proper man-overboard position. Again, I rode up and over the wave, from one trough to the next. This pattern repeated for the next five rapids.

Finally, the rushing, tumultuous rapids were over, replaced by the steady gurgling we'd enjoyed further upstream. The drill was done. And, amazingly, I'd come through it alive. My float was done. I began kicking my legs, moving my arms, to swim toward shore. The rest of the group was there to greet me, each of them clapping at my performance.

None of them had witnessed my indecision, my frozen state, my abject fear that day. But I knew how I'd responded—and to this day, I have never forgotten it. In the aftermath of the drill, I realized that being paralyzed there on the banks of the Rogue River had been a much worse experience than the actual drill itself. Never would I freeze up like that again, I vowed.

A few hours later, our group stood on the edge of a rocky cliff we'd hiked up to. The river flowed about six stories beneath us.

"We're going to repel down this cliff," one of the leaders boomed, his voice competing with the wind as it tried whisking his words away. "Can I have a volunteer to go first?"

I didn't hesitate a moment. My hand shot into the air.

"I'll go first," I announced.

Outward Bound

Yes, I was frightened. But I pushed past the fear. I acknowledged my anxiety, faced it, and dealt with it. For me, the fear of repelling down the cliff was more bearable than the fear of freezing up, as I had done during the man-overboard drill, and being stranded there alone. It was the lesser of two fears.

I learned that day that it is not unusual to experience fear, but what is important is that you acknowledge that fear and have a plan to deal with it. I didn't abolish fear from my life that day. I still get nervous, worried, fearful. But I did decide that day to not be ashamed of fear—to instead recognize it for what it is, take the plunge, and do my best to persevere through it.

Outward Bound turned out to be an inward revelation for me.

SEVENTEEN

Seagulls

Persisting to a Fault

Seagulls and I do not get along.

My relationship with seagulls went off the deep end when I was thirteen years old. We were vacationing on Cape Cod, on its southeastern corner near the town of Chatham, where I loved running over the many sand dunes. On one of my spirited runs, I must have gone too close to a seagull nest because the bird started attacking me with a vengeance.

I was young enough that this experience really scared me. Seagulls are big birds, some over two feet long, and a threatening size to a still growing youth. And when they are upset or agitated, they can be very aggressive and attack ferociously. They swoop down and aim for your head with their stout, long bills. Out on the open dunes with little protection, such an attack is especially frightening to a kid.

In the following twenty-five years, that experience remained an unpleasant memory, kept mostly in the far reaches of my mind—until one of my visits to Anchorage. I was returning from one of my week-long salmon-fishing float trips on an Alaskan river when I checked into one of the better hotels in Anchorage for the night. I usually would lay over for one night in the city before catching a plane back to Seattle the next day. This allowed me time to wash my clothes and get cleaned up—which, after seven days in the wilds of Alaska, is a priority.

This particular time I was not feeling tip-top. My stomach was bothering me, but I refused even to consider that I might be sick. Having checked into the hotel, I was squirming, still uncomfortable. I had to do something to make my stomach feel better. *Perhaps jogging would help!* I thought. I hadn't done much in the way of exercise during the fishing trip and hadn't gone running in a week. So I put on my jogging clothes and headed through the hotel's revolving front door and began my jog on West Third Avenue, one of Anchorage's main streets. Stores line one side of the street, and a sidewalk and railing the other. The railing provides protection from a cliff that drops down to the waters of Cook Inlet below. It's a beautiful scene. And as I jogged, I had a perfect view of the harbor over the railing.

Soon I noticed I had company. Overhead a seagull kept up with me, but it obviously did not have good intentions. Big white seagull excrements landed on the sidewalk on all sides of me. Either the gull had very poor aim and equally bad luck, or it had excellent target skills and was giving me plenty of indications that I should go away. Major drops of seagull waste continued just to miss me as I jogged along West Third, trying to mind my own business and hoping to make my stomach feel better. *Why is this seagull trying to poop on me?* I asked myself. *What did I do to it? There can't be a seagull's nest on one of the main streets, can there?*

I began to jog a little faster, trying to shake the gull. Yes, I thought I could outrun a bird. Talk about a challenge! As I increased my pace and became more concerned about my "companion," my heart rate increased and my breathing got shorter.

Given my history with seagulls, I tensed up. I knew what it could do if it stopped playing with me and got serious. I began glancing upward to check on the location of the seagull...frequently...about every ten seconds. I wanted to get rid of this thing!

No such luck. Like the seagull from my youth, this one, too, began swooping toward me, going after my head. I felt as if I were in a World

I felt as if I were in a World War II movie with Japanese planes dive-bombing me

War II movie with Japanese planes dive-bombing me. I prayed that this plane was not operated by a kamikaze pilot.

Oh, my gosh.

I picked up my speed. No longer jogging, I was running as fast as I could. Panic had taken over. And that may explain why I continued on my course. Turn back? I didn't even consider it. Once I set a goal, I carry on, attacking seagull notwithstanding. Evidently, the seagull was of an equally determined temperament as it gave no indication of letting up in its attacks. On the contrary, my running seemed only to intensify its response.

To protect myself, I began falling to the ground each time the seagull swooped down to get me. Whenever it would dive-bomb, I too would dive to the ground, just in the nick of time. Then I would get up, quickly recover, and start running again. I repeated this again. And again. And again.

All of this on one of the main streets in Anchorage! What entertainment I must have provided to the citizenry and tourists.

This jog certainly was more of a workout than I'd planned. I had a lot of stamina. I was in good condition. And I could run forever—or so I thought. Yet a lowly gull was showing me otherwise. I couldn't keep up this dance. My breathing was labored. My muscles were revolting. And my whole body was shaking.

I thought I was going to die because I just couldn't run any further. Nor could I stop. Just like in Alfred Hitchcock's *The Birds*, this bird would peck me to death. I started hyperventilating.

Just then a police patrol car approached and came right up to me. It stopped. I went over to the warm hood of the car and leaned on it, severely bent over, trying to catch my breath. The officer kept his car running.

Before I could begin to explain to the officer what was going on, he said to me, "This happens all the time. Don't worry. The car's engine scares the seagulls away."

The officer was very patient, allowing me time to catch my breath. I must have looked like a ghost, scared white and not believing what

I had just been through. The whole experience seemed unreal and made no sense at all.

And the juxtaposition of my just completed fishing trip made the scene even more incongruous. I had finished seven days of floating one of the wildest rivers of Alaska, totally removed from civilization, surrounded by nature at its most pristine and dangerous, always on guard for grizzly bears. I had survived that environment just fine. But upon my return to the relative safety of civilization, jogging down a major street in Alaska's most populous city, I had one of the scariest, most heart-stopping encounters with nature in my adult life.

Finally the officer said to me, "May I give you a lift back to your hotel in the patrol car?"

At this point, pride took over. How was I going to explain this to anybody? I had to be given a ride in a police vehicle to protect me from a bird on one of the main streets in Anchorage? How incredibly absurd! No way!

So I thanked him very much and said that I would jog back.

"If you don't mind," he said, "I'll follow behind you in the patrol car, just to make sure you make it back safely."

I didn't argue. I just started jogging ver-r-r-y slowly. As I went along, I tried to figure out what had just happened to me and what in the world seagulls have against me.

After I returned to the hotel, still shaken from the incident, I realized that my stomach still didn't feel good. Apparently a jog was not the solution to my stomach problems.

✳ ✳ ✳

And the moral of the story?

No matter how determined you are, you can't out-persevere a seagull.

EIGHTEEN
Sleep Disorders

Keeping Priorities Straight

All my adult life I have had a tendency to fall asleep at the drop of a hat, and often in the most inappropriate places and at the most inopportune times.

Playing Bridge

In my late twenties, my first wife, Ellen, and I would often visit Brian and Nancy Baxter's house for the evening, where we would have dinner, drinks, and then play bridge together—if I lasted that long.

The most infamous of my "fades" happened one night when all of us were sitting around the card table, beginning our bidding. I started out with a bid of "one club." Nancy, sitting to my left, then bid "one heart," followed by my wife (and partner for that round) bidding "two clubs." Brian, sitting to my right, then followed with "two hearts."

At this point the bidding was back to me. Everyone turned to find me breathing softly, head forward, chin on my chest, and eyes closed. "He's asleep," Ellen said. My cards had fallen out of my hands and were scattered, face up, on the table in front of me. I had fallen asleep, sitting in my chair, playing cards, in the time it had taken to go around the table just once for bidding.

Driving

I have dozed at the wheel too many times. Enough said. It's very scary.

At the Movies

I am notorious for sleeping during movies. It is unusual if I do not fall asleep for at least some portion of a movie. Rarely do I catch the entire movie. Whenever I get into a movie theater, lean back in my chair, and relax as the lights go down…oh boy, do I ever struggle to stay awake.

Needless to say, this can prove quite a hindrance when it comes to dating. My first date with Ellen was at a movie in which I fell asleep. After the movie I tried to explain to her that it happened all the time, that it had nothing to do with *her*. Right. A tough sell that I would end up having to make many times over the years.

At the Theater

The worst sleeping incident occurred not at the movie theater but at a performing arts theater. I was in Los Angeles on a double date with an important congressman's chief of staff. We both had blind dates and were on our way to see *The Phantom of the Opera* at the Music Center.

Phantom does not lend itself to dozing. It is lively, noisy, and full of action. But I found a way to do it. No sooner had the first act started than I was sound asleep in my seat. I slept through the entire first act.

At intermission I told myself that I wasn't going to let that happen again. I went to the snack bar to buy a chocolate brownie and bag of Peanut M&M's to help me stay awake. I was *determined* not to fall asleep again.

But despite the good nap I had just had during the first act, and despite the loads of sugar and caffeine I'd just consumed during my chocolate binge, I still managed to fall asleep again. I slept through the entire second act—which was the final act. I missed the entire performance.

On Airplanes

I do not know what it is about airplanes, but as soon as I sit down in one, I am very relaxed and can easily fall asleep. Often times I will be dead asleep before the plane even leaves the gate, much less takes off.

The most embarrassing story of my falling asleep on an airplane happened on St. Patrick's Day in 1989. I had partied all afternoon and into the early evening in San Francisco—and I'd had way too much to drink. Later I raced to the airport to catch a late flight to Seattle. I got on the plane and immediately fell asleep ("passed out" might be a better term). The next thing I knew, I was in Seattle, with a stewardess shaking my shoulder, asking me to wake up. I looked around the plane to see that nobody was on it. The entire plane had already disembarked, and I was the only one left. If she hadn't woken me, I probably would still be sleeping in the seat on that plane!

❊ ❊ ❊

But none of these stories compare to what happened to me when I started to fly to the Philippines on a regular basis.

I decided to start my transportation consulting business, Transportation Solutions, in the mid 90s. I had no clients to begin with. But as with every other start-up in my life, I had a lot of energy to devote to it and I believed that I would land some clients, having recently completed work as the one in charge of transportation in Los Angeles. However, deep inside of me was much nervousness and doubt about being able to get my first contract. I asked myself, *Will my business get off the ground? Can I build a respectable business?*

In an unusual turn of events, during my extended trip to Southeast Asia after leaving the LA metro job, I had been introduced to the leaders of the Ayala Corporation, the largest land developer in the Philippines. It was concerned that its land holdings in the central business district in Manila and suburban housing developments were losing value because of the catastrophic congestion that crawled throughout the Manila metropolitan area. Ayala saw passenger rail as a solution to the area's congestion problems, as well as to maintaining and enhancing its property values, providing easier access between home and work. Since I had earned the reputation as the man who had brought rail back to Los Angeles after a forty-year absence, I was asked if I would be available to assist the company on a consulting basis.

I responded that indeed I would, knowing that Ayala could be my first big client for my new company. *Yes!*

But then I saw a problem. Ayala wanted me full time in Manila for the next three years. *Yikes!* I said to myself, *What about the kids?*

I had always been determined to be the best father to my son and daughter. My divorce had not changed my resolve. I remained committed to my children and took seriously the agreed-upon 50-50 custody of the children. In practice, this worked out to two weeks a month with me, and two weeks a month with their mom.

A full-time obligation in the Philippines would severely compromise my commitment to the children—possibly eliminate time with them for all but a few weeks of the year. *How could I meet my obligations to my kids and also get my consulting business off the ground?* I was torn. This was the break that I was looking for. This contract would instantly put my company in business. Yet, I was determined to be the best dad in the world for my kids. They were eleven and nine, and I knew I would never recapture the time lost during these years. I was not going to miss this time with them, nor would they miss out on time with me.

The decision was easy: The kids came first.

I emailed a proposal to the leaders of the Ayala Corporation. I explained my dilemma, that I would like to do this, but my children and my obligations as a father came first. I said that the only way that I could accept the offer was if I could continue to meet my responsibilities with the kids for two weeks of every month. My offer was that at Ayala's expense, I would fly back and forth to the states every two weeks so I could be with the kids.

I punched the "send" button on my computer. I knew in my heart that I had made the right decision. But I could not help mourning the loss of my first major contract, the one that would have lifted my nascent business into adulthood. I knew that the company would refuse my proposal.

I was wrong! Dead wrong!

General Douglas MacArthur, "I shall return"
Corregidor, Philippines
(Kelsey, Guy, and Neil Peterson)

To my utter surprise Ayala accepted my proposal as written. I could not believe it,

I had the expertise needed, and I believe, my unusual demand actually worked in my favor. I did not fully appreciate at the time, but I have since come to understand the importance that family and children have in the Philippine culture. The importance I attached to my family and my role as father struck a chord that resonated with the company. And Ayala responded.

The good news was twofold. I had secured a significant three-year contract that instantly put my fledgling company in business. And I would continue to parent my kids two weeks every month.

The bad news seemed minor at the time. While I realized that flying across the Pacific every two weeks would be taxing, I had no idea how brutal the impact of the travel would be on me over the long haul. On the first day of each month, I would fly to the Philippines—board in Seattle, change planes in San Francisco or Los Angeles, then fly to Seoul, Korea, and on to Manila. Occasionally I would get a nonstop flight from Los Angeles to Manila, but in either case, it was approximately twenty-four hours from door to door and fifteen and one half hours of actual flight time. And since I was crossing the International Date Line, there was a time change of sixteen hours.

After three years I was a walking zombie.

My horrendous commuting schedule had greatly amplified my sleep problems, and I had had enough. Finally, at the age of fifty-four, I signed up for testing at Providence Hospital's sleep disorder clinic in Seattle.

The process was quite elaborate and thorough.

First I met with Dr. Sensabaugh. He explained to me all the steps of the testing process.

Second, I had to keep a "sleep diary" for three weeks. I had to record when I went to bed, when I fell asleep, when I woke up, when I dreamt, and if I got up during the night and for what reasons. It was a very thorough diary.

Third, I had to fill out an unbelievably lengthy questionnaire. It took hours to complete.

Fourth, I had to go back to the doctor's office to be interviewed by a medical assistant. She was armed with my sleep diary and my completed questionnaire, and during our meeting…yes, I fell asleep sitting in the chair while I was being questioned by the medical assistant. *Not a good sign*, I said to myself when I woke up, although I certainly had given proof of the extent of my problem. Still I wondered, *Am I screwed up or what?*

Fifth, I checked into the hospital for an overnight stay so my sleep patterns could be monitored in person.

What an experience this was. Wow! They put electrodes all over me, especially on my head. Twenty different color tubes, most of them close to two-feet long, were attached to my head, held on by some special glue. When I went down to the hospital cafeteria to get some food, the other patients there were visibly shaken, shocked, and taken aback by what they saw: a guy with multicolored tubes coming out of his head. I looked scary.

The hospital bedroom was something to behold. Not only did it have machines that connected to all of these tubes, but it also looked like a TV studio. Cameras everywhere! The medical personnel obviously weren't going to be satisfied with just the information coming from the electrodes; they also wanted to see real live sleeping in action. Reality TV!

Outside of my room was the most elaborate, high-tech station you could imagine. It looked like a TV production room (to match the TV studio that was my room!).

It also reminded me of an air traffic control tower—or at least what I imagined an air traffic control tower must look like. There were many screens, graphs, charts, monitors, and devices…and staff people, sitting in chairs, dressed in white doctor's coats, all with the intent of watching me sleep and monitoring my sleep patterns.

The night passed. They got their data. And I was discharged from the hospital the next morning.

The sixth and final step was for me to meet again with Dr. Sensabaugh and get his evaluation, analysis, and recommendations.

This whole process had taken weeks. They had tremendous information on my sleeping habits at this point, and I was anxiously looking forward to the meeting to find out what was wrong with me. Was it narcolepsy? Sleep apnea? Something I had never heard of? And could it be fixed? Would I ever be able to watch a movie like a normal person?.

Dr Sensabaugh welcomed me into his office. He said he knew it had been a long process, and he thanked me for cooperating with the data-gathering techniques.

I acknowledged his comments and jumped right to the heart of the matter. "So," I asked, "what did you find?"

Dr. Sensabaugh said that, in all of his years, he had never seen someone as screwed up as I was. My body was so messed up that he couldn't even diagnose the problem.

"It's a first for me," he said. "I've never had this happen before."

Great. I'm a freak, I thought to myself.

He told me that my constant travel back and forth to the Philippines had just thrown my body for a loop and that we needed to give it time to settle back into to a more normal pattern.

"We can redo the tests in the future," he added, "but right now, I'm sorry to say, I can't make heads or tails out of the data I have in front of me. Come back when you're more normal, and I'll do it all over again for no additional cost. Okay, Neil?"

I nodded in agreement.

But I never went back.

✳ ✳ ✳

Was the grueling travel schedule worth the worsening of my sleep problems? You bet! I got that first contract I needed to establish my credibility outside the governmental arena. But most important, I shared those three years with my children as I had promised them. I ushered them into adolescence. I was with them in moments that otherwise would have been lost. And I let them know I would always be in their lives, regardless of the cost on my part.

Since then, my sleeping problem has abated somewhat.

But I still fall asleep—usually when I sit down to relax.

NINETEEN
Snowboarding

Staying Young (at Heart)

I took up snowboarding in 1995, at the age of fifty-one. "Why?" you may ask. I wanted to be with my kids. My son, Guy, was eleven and my daughter, Kelsey, was nine years old at the time. They wanted to try this new sport, seemingly even "cooler" than skiing and all the rage among their friends at school.

My thought process was that if the kids wanted to do it, I would help them in every way I could. I have always encouraged their involvement in athletics and sports competition. I am a big believer that participation in sports is good for you not only in developing physically and mentally but also in learning many of the life skills and values that will serve you later no matter what situation you may find yourself in.

I took them to the local Fiorini Sports store north of downtown Seattle to rent their first snowboards and boots. One of my rules with the kids was that I initially would support their athletic endeavors by renting equipment. When, and if, they showed me they were truly serious about the sport and dedicated to it, I would step up and purchase the equipment for them, but only then, not in the beginning.

I would not spend money on equipment for what might be only a temporary enthusiasm.

In addition to renting the boards and boots, I made sure they had the right kind of goggles, gloves, pants, and jackets. Unfortunately, I could not rent these items.

I also arranged for lessons so that they would learn the right techniques from the beginning. Although they could have taken the ski school bus from Fiorini Sports to the mountains, I wanted this to be time that I would spend with them. So, instead, I drove them to the ski areas on the weekends—Snoqualmie Summit, Stevens Pass, or Alpental. Depending upon which ski area we went to, the drive was anywhere from one to two hours each way from Seattle. That was a lot of time with my children.

✳ ✳ ✳

When I got the kids to the ski area and off to their lessons, all of a sudden I realized that I had a whole lot of time with nothing to do. *What am I going to do for the next seven hours as I wait for them?* I wondered. Sitting around the lodge sipping hot chocolate was not for me. I cannot stand sitting and waiting. I love to be doing something, especially sports.

Then I thought, *If I learn how to snowboard, I can be on the slopes with my kids. It will be another way that we can spend time together.*

But wait, I thought. *Didn't I promise myself, after my serious skiing accident some twelve years ago, that I would give up skiing?* I had spent six long months in rehabilitation after severing the medial collateral, posterior and anterior cruciate ligaments of my right knee skiing at Whistler in British Columbia. *What am I thinking about?*

In addition, I reflected, *I do not see any adults, much less anyone over fifty years of age, with a snowboard!* Most adults thought snowboarding was crazy. At the time, many ski areas would not even allow boarding on their slopes. It was definitely a generational phenomenon.

Nevertheless, I mused, *if I am going to make this effort to help get the kids started in snowboarding, then why don't I do the same for me?*

I signed up for lessons, too.

NINETEEN
SNOWBOARDING

❋ ❋ ❋

After noting the dearth of more mature adults on snowboards, the next thing I noticed was the difference in connecting my boots to the snowboard versus stepping into skis. One foot was no problem, but the gyrations and contortions required to get the second boot secured at a right angle to the first severely challenged my body. Already I could tell that this was a sport invented with young, flexible bodies in mind.

My best solution to this problem was to find a bench, sit on it, bend over, and snap the boots in place. This worked well. Unfortunately, there are not many benches on a ski slope. Just the effort to secure my boots to the snowboard was exhausting. I quickly realized that my body did not bend the way it used to, or was supposed to. Once my boots were secured to the snowboard, the effort to get up, to stand up on the board challenged every natural instinct I had.

For example, to stand up, if you have no handy bench upon which you have been sitting, you need to face into the hill. That is likely not the position you have been in while securing boots to board. So you must flip over somehow from a position with back to hill to one with face to hill. Remember, while you do this, your feet are strapped at right angles to each other on the board. This is definitely not a sport for fifty-plus-year-olds. Once facing into the hill, you lift yourself up with your legs and arms pushing against the snow until you are upright, still facing uphill, and leaning slightly into the hill.

All that I did! I felt I had made significant progress, and I had not even tried going anywhere. I said to myself, *Wait! How is this going to work? I want to go downhill; I need to face downhill.* But I was standing facing uphill.

At first, you are taught to slip slide slowly down the hill.

You slip down the hill, your back facing downhill, the front of your body leaning into the hill. When you want to slip, you subtlety shift or transfer your weight from your toes with the edge of the board into the snow to the middle of your feet with less focus on the edge of the board into the side of the slope. To rest, you can fall to your knees as the uphill edge of your snowboard is firmly stuck on the slope.

Not bad so far, I mumbled to myself. I did wonder how I would manage when I would be facing downhill and then when I would want to turn and then when I would be speeding down the mountain.

Unlike skiing, snowboarding involves no poles—there is nothing to use to help make a turn or help keep your balance.

The next step is to try the same exercise, but this time facing downhill, slip sliding down the hill and stopping by shifting the weight to your heels, which in turn digs into the snow and slope. All the while you are bending your knees, keeping your upper body positioned toward the downhill fall line.

Next come the turns, which are similar to those in skiing. You head down the fall line, briefly and subtlely shift your weight from the heels to the toes, or vice versa, depending upon whether you are traversing left to right or right to left across the slope.

The first time I tried this, I took a *big header.* That is, when moving at a good rate of speed, you crash to the ground and your back or chest bangs on the snow. It is jolting. But the real killer is the slightly delayed response of the head, which often whips itself onto the snow after the upper body has taken the initial hit. This delayed, almost whip-lash banging of the head against the snow gets your attention real fast. And banging it into hard-packed snow especially shocks the old body.

All snowboarders wear helmets for a reason.

My daughter and I were in the same class. The first two days of lessons were difficult for me; they were easy for her. I was having trouble getting it; she was a natural. I must have fallen a hundred times; I was too busy falling and getting up to notice if she ever hit the snow. But I kept at it; and so did she.

On the morning of the third day, I woke up with plans to have another day of snowboarding lessons. However, as I attempted to roll over and get out of bed, my body did not respond. At all. My poor bruised, tired, stretched body was yelling *no mas* and had shut down.

✳ ✳ ✳

On the fourth day, ever the determined sports enthusiast and parent, I was once again back on the slopes. A massage and sleep

Dad, let's go snowboarding
Kelsey, Guy (front), and Neil

and time in the hot tub can work amazing wonders on a body that is not responding.

On that day, I learned that aside from getting your snowboarding boots on and in addition to learning how to negotiate the slopes, the next most difficult task is getting on and off the chairlifts.

Usually I am the only over-twenty-something in the chairlift line with a snowboard, and it is obvious that I am not comfortable riding on it. To get on the chair, you must wait in line, which moves at a slow but constant pace. When you ski, you are standing upright on your two skis, sliding forward a foot at a time. No problem. But when you are a snowboarder, you unbuckle one of your boots from the snowboard and hop forward with one foot still secured to the board. The problem with this is that your two feet (one on packed snow, the other strapped to the board) are not pointing in the same direction. No! In fact, the foot strapped to the board is facing towards you. That's right. Your strapped right foot points not forward but 90 degrees to the left. Egads! Not only does it look odd, but it feels awkward and hurts like crazy. This is not a natural position for any fifty-year-old, even ones who practice tai chi every morning. Standing, waiting, hopping in line for the chairlift was one of those moments when I silently asked myself, *Why am I doing this? This is not fun.* Snowboarding is obviously a sport meant to separate the young from the others. But even though I felt like a reject from Cirque de Soleil, I was not about to remain on the sidelines while my kids whizzed down the slopes.

Onward I hopped.

But as agonizing as getting on the chairlift is, it is nothing compared to the sheer terror of getting off the chair at the end of its ride up the mountain. Getting off was an absolute disaster. The only issue I had was which direction I was going to fall.

✳ ✳ ✳

The good news about snowboarding is that it is difficult to hurt your knees, which was my main concern since I did not want a repeat of my knee injury. The bad news, however, is that the sport is very hard on the upper body. The back and the chest take most of the punishment. But the real surprise, at least for me, has been the impact on my head. More often than not, every time I fall, my chest or back takes the initial impact but my head, in delayed reaction, whiplashes into the snow or ice. In the last twelve years of snowboarding, I have had three concussions—and that is while wearing a helmet!!

✳ ✳ ✳

Still to this day the kids and I go snowboarding at least every two years for a week. And yes, I have gotten to the point where I am decent going down the slopes, albeit the green (or easiest) runs. Once in a great while, I will attempt a more difficult blue run. And yes, I have solved the problem of getting my boots secured on my snowboard: I have my kids put them on for me while I stand up and watch the scenery. Works like a charm, and I am not exhausted from the effort.

My original goal of doing this to spend more time with the kids did not work because they are so good that they do not want to board with me. They will take, maybe, one obligatory first run of the day with their dad, but then they are off on their own, and I don't see them until the day is over. In the evenings, we do gather together, so the week spent snowboarding does give me time with them that I would not otherwise have had.

The kids realize that there are very few dads anywhere near my age who stand in the chairlift line strapped to their snowboard. I am sure they know their dad does it for them. And I suspect that they even hold a little bit of pride in their dad for trying so hard. Who knows? Maybe they are secretly proud to be their Dad's kids.

✳ ✳ ✳

The moral of this story is that, if you want to spend time with your kids, sometimes you need to give a lot of effort—and be willing to take a few bumps and bruises along the way.

TWENTY

Unstoppable

Knowing When to Take a Break

As the cruise ship pulled away from the dock, I stood on the aft deck, looking for the last time at the many colored tin houses, nestled on the hills of Valparaiso. In the sparkling sun, the scene had a vibrant magic.

I hated to leave the city, so rich with history, located on the Pacific coast of Chile, an hour's drive from Santiago, the nation's capital. Coffee shops were bursting at the seams with aspiring writers and poets. Music seemed to echo from every corner. People filled the streets in animated conversation at all hours of the day. The city had a funky, almost Bohemian feel to it.

For two days, it had been a fun and reflective place for me and a far cry from what was in store for me for the next two weeks. I had auditioned for and been selected to be a "dance host" on a Norwegian Cruise Lines cruise ship. The two-week cruise from Santiago, Chile, to Buenos Aires, Argentina, would include Patagonia, the Falklands, as well as Cape Horn and the Strait of Magellan. Although it was December and therefore summer, we could expect to encounter winds and rain as we rounded the most southern tip of South America.

What is a "dance host"? Many cruise ships hire gentlemen who are accomplished dancers to be available to dance with women. If you have ever seen the movie *Out to Sea* with Jack Lemmon and Walter Matthau, you may have some insight into what the life of a dance host on a cruise ship is like.

Our typical daily schedule involved being on the dance floor at 6 o'clock every evening and dancing until midnight. We danced four of the six hours, and a theater production filled up the remaining two hours. We never took a break. We danced to every single tune.

Our dress code varied, depending on the theme that night on the cruise ship. One night might be the 50's, another California casual with sport jacket but no tie, and several were formal with black or white tuxedos. In addition to being very well dressed, we were always expected to wear a smile.

And, yes, there were some rules that we had to abide by. We could not dance with just one woman. We could not dance more than one dance in a row with one woman. We could not become attached to a particular woman. We could not cross the threshold of a woman's room. Nor were we allowed to have a woman cross the threshold of our room.

Rules, rules, rules! But that is another story.

One of the benefits of being a dance host and working only evenings was that my days were free and clear. I could do what I wanted.

Our first day on the cruise was a "sea day," but our second was to be our first port of call. Puerto Montt in the Lake District of Chile was where we would tie up for the day. People were free to disembark and explore the town and surrounding area as they wished.

Many people signed up for "shore excursions," which were organized trips into the surrounding countryside. Some were culturally oriented, some shopping oriented. But there was always one that was focused on adventure sports. The one that day was called "zip-lining."

I had never done it but had vaguely heard about it. My image was something similar to Tarzan swinging—literally "zipping"—from tree to tree in the forest harnessed to some kind of steel cable.

UNSTOPPABLE

Without hesitation I said to myself, *I'll do it. A new adventure, something different. I need the exercise. It will be fun.* I had signed up as soon as I had heard about it.

That morning all who had signed up for zip-lining headed onto a tour bus ready for the hour plus drive to the base of Orsono Volcano, a beautiful, perfectly inverted cone, standing guard over Lake Llanquihue.

However, there was one problem—the weather. It was raining. *Pouring.* It was raining so hard that the four-wheel-drive army jeeps used to transport us up the mountain were unable to negotiate the rugged road. Half of the group decided to give up and return to the cruise ship. The rest of us decided to hike up the mountain, tracing the trail that the jeep was to have traversed.

Once we reached the section of the forest that marked the beginning of the zip-lining experience, we received a briefing on what to expect, how to put on the harness, how to put our feet up when we reached the end of each leg of the zip-line, and how to slow down by wearing a leather glove, grabbing hold of the steel cable and pulling down on the cable to create friction.

We climbed up ladders to a small platform surrounding the trunk of a large tree. Standing perhaps one third of the way up the mountain and perhaps fifty feet above the floor of the forest on a narrow wooden platform, I was nervous as I secured my helmet. Climbing into the harness, with one strap around each leg and one around my chest, I paid particular attention to the carabineer that connected my harness with the rope that in turn connected with a pulley suspended from the steel cable. I wanted to assure myself that the hardware was strong enough to hold a 220-pound person of my size.

But the real surprise came when I looked up to see where the steel cable went. The cable stretched across a deep ravine that was as wide as five football fields. The distance was so great that the cable sagged, drooping like a "U." I wondered how I was going to gain enough momentum from gravity. Was I going to be able to traverse the ravine? Was my speed going to be enough to make it up the tail end of the "U" to the next tree? I worried that I was so heavy that I would get stuck in the middle of the U-shaped cable and be stranded with no obvious escape route.

Yes, I was scared. I was the heaviest person in our group, and I was not sure that I would make it to the next tree. I asked the staff person Enrique, "How many of these ravine crossings are we going to have before we are at the bottom of the mountain?"

Enrique answered, "This is the first of eleven crossings."

I added, "Is there any point where you can get off the zip-lining and walk back down the mountain?"

"No," Enrique said, "you are committed now. There is no turning back."

I then asked him, "Will I be able to make it to the next tree? Am I too heavy to make it up the last part of the cable?"

"*No problema*," he responded. "The heavier you are, the greater speed you generate when you slide down the steel cable."

"Don't worry," he added. "You can slow down your speed by using the leather glove to pull down on the cable, creating friction." He demonstrated how. He stressed that you really had to apply pressure. Particularly, he added, because the cable is wet, the amount of friction that you can generate will be reduced.

"In addition," he continued, "we have an arrester system so that if you are going too fast coming into the next tree, we have a man on duty with a device that will brake you in plenty of time before you hit the tree. And the tree has padding wrapped around its trunk. So don't worry."

Famous last words, I thought to myself. But then I caught myself and started some self-talk, saying, *Come on, Neil, suck it up. Many people have done this before, and they survived. Others in our group are going to do it. And they don't appear to be scared. How embarrassing it would be to quit. No way.*

When it was my turn, I took off on my zip-line, harnessed in, with my gloved right hand cupped around the cable. I was worried about not having enough speed to make it up the tail end of the U and getting stuck and stranded in the middle of the ravine. At the same time

"No," Enrique said, "you are committed now. There is no turning back"

I was worried about getting up too much speed and slamming into the next tree.

Off I flew into the wild blue yonder. I gathered speed as I hurtled down the cable toward the middle of the huge ravine, and just as Enrique had said, I had plenty of momentum to continue on up the last half of the U. And more. I realized that I was moving so fast that I would go well past that first tree.

Holy cow!

I started to pull on the cable with my glove, but it didn't do any good. I pulled down harder. No luck. The cable was so wet from the rain that my efforts to slow myself down were futile.

In front of me was a huge tree, getting bigger by the second, and I was aimed right at it. Barreling down the steel cable, I was like a missile, traveling at a speed beyond my control and zooming in on my target. And I continued to gain speed with the velocity of the descent.

The wind screeched through my helmet. The scenery flew by in one solid blur. And the tree trunk only grew greater. My heart was pounding faster and faster, louder and louder. I felt like Evel Knievel, flying through the air, but with no place to land, just a huge tree trunk in front of me. I could do nothing but watch and wait and hope beyond hope.

The tree was almost upon me. I braced myself because unless the arrester safety brake worked I was about to slam feet first into the tree. I extended my feet out in front of me, and in an attempt to do something, I bent my knees to cushion the blow.

Within seconds of reaching the tree, to my relief, I saw the staff person holding the safety brake. *Yes! I'll be okay*, I thought as I watched him pull it. And then, *Oh, no!* as I continued to race down and…

WHACK!

I slammed into the tree trunk. I crashed to the narrow wooden platform in a heap. And I didn't move. I felt as if I had been hit by a truck.

The staff person immediately came to my aid, asking if I was OK. I had just rammed into a solid object at an incredible speed, but I assured him that I was just fine. Others quickly gathered around to see the result of my encounter with the tree.

"Holy cow!"

When I attempted to get up, I realized that maybe I was not OK after all. My legs hurt from the impact. Particularly my left leg. Especially my left knee. Ohhh….

I had no way out of the zip-line but one. Once I had started, I had to go the eleven segments. So I did, but each segment represented a significant effort to reduce the chance that there would be a repeat of the first disaster. Eventually I made it down all eleven, got back on the tour bus, and returned to the ship.

My cabin on the ship was right next to the medical facility. I stopped in to talk to the doctor.

I told him what had happened and that I was in a lot of pain.

He looked me over and gave me two Ibuprofen. He asked me to let him know if the pain continued.

After a shower and dinner, I assumed my dancing duties for four hours that night. But my leg continued to bother me.

The next day I revisited the doctor and told him that the leg still hurt. He gave me four Ibuprofen.

The next night I took up my position and performed my dance duties as assigned.

The third day I again walked into the doctor's office complaining. This time he gave me an elastic knee brace.

I tried the elastic brace that night, but the pain persisted.

I danced for four hours every night for each of the remaining nights on the two-week cruise.

After arriving in Buenos Aires, my two kids joined me, having taken the long plane flight from Seattle. The three of us spent the next two weeks exploring Patagonia, Buenos Aires, and Iguaçu Falls. We hiked the glaciers in southern Argentina. We hiked for several days in the Torres del Paine National Park in Chile. We hiked for two days exploring Iguaçu Falls on the border of Argentina and Brazil. And we spent a few days at the end in Buenos Aires taking Argentine tango lessons.

When I finally returned to the States after my four weeks in Chile, Argentina, Brazil, and Patagonia, I decided that I should have another doctor take a look at my leg. It still was giving me pain.

*Torres del Paine National Park, Patagonia, Chile
(Guy, Kelsey, and Neil)*

The results of an MRI showed that my left leg was broken. I had suffered a compression fracture just below my knee.

The doctor said to stay off the leg for four weeks. Well, it was a little late for that, considering that it had been four weeks since I had broken it.

Lesson learned? I am unstoppable. I danced and continued my life for four weeks on a broken leg.

And, as far as zip-lines are concerned? I should have realized that I was unstoppable.

*Glacier National Park, Patagonia, Argentina
(Kelsey, Guy, and Neil)*

*Perito Moreno Glacier
(Guy, Neil, and Kelsey)*

The Rogue Wave

Finding the Strength to Persevere

Although summer's late afternoon sun still gave light and warmth, I knew from the lengthening shadows in the cave that evening's chill would soon creep in. And hypothermia would quickly follow.

NO! I couldn't hold such thoughts. I pushed them far back into the recesses of my mind once more, just as I'd done repeatedly over the last 9 hours.

Stay focused, Neil. Keep your cool and stay focused...

With me were three "twenty-somethings": my son Guy (22), my daughter Kelsey (20), and my nephew Tim (28). Like cornered animals, we perched on two narrow pieces of driftwood, wedged awkwardly into a coastal cave's wall, four stories above the churning waters of the Pacific Ocean.

At sixty-three, I was the older leader of the group, but my years of wisdom and experience hardly mattered now. I'd dealt with grizzly bears while salmon fishing in Alaska. I'd walked out of a whiteout when summiting Mt. Baker. I'd spent my life facing adventures, thrilled with the challenge to survive each new danger. Yet none came close to what the four of us now faced. I felt incredibly ill-equipped to handle our precarious situation and at a loss for a way out. Meanwhile, Death waited patiently round the corner as time for a solution drained away.

✻ ✻ ✻

Almost fourteen hours earlier, at 3:30 a.m. on a cool June morning, I, along with the rest of my gang, had been breaking camp at Thrasher Cove. As I shook sand out of my tent and stuffed gear into my 50-pound pack, the misting rain looked like pins falling from the sky in the light of my headlamp.

We were hiking the West Coast Trail, which hugs the southwest coast of Vancouver Island, British Columbia. Seamen who had been washed ashore in shipwrecks one hundred years before had forged the 75-kilometer trail (approximately the length of Rhode Island) as a way to escape the "Graveyard of the Pacific," as this section of coastline had come to be called.

Our night at Thrasher Cove had been an adventure in and of itself. The high tide coming in that night had threatened to sweep our camp away, and everyone but me had to move their tents to stay out of the water's reach. It was a fitting cap to an already tiring day—our first in a planned seven-day hike. That day's hike had been grueling, and we were beat, especially after the 52 story descent we'd tackled to get down to Thrasher Cove.

But as far as I was concerned, it was worth it. I'd been looking forward to this hike for years, the chance to add yet another outdoor adventure to my lifelong list—"West Coast Trail," right up there with hiking Torres del Paine National Park in Chile and rafting and hiking the Colorado River and Grand Canyon.

Even more important, it was an opportunity to spend time with my kids. Growing up, my dad had never given me the time or attention I had needed. He had never even found it in himself to play a simple game of catch with me in the backyard! Early on, I had made a vow that my kids would always get the love and attention that my dad had never showed me. Even in their adulthood, I made a point of setting aside weeks each year for trips with Kelsey and Guy.

*left to right, Joe Ellis, Guy Peterson, Kelsey Peterson,
Tim Kniffin, Neil*

✳ ✳ ✳

In the cave, we were scared. But we each pretended we were fine, not letting on to the others how close to death and hopeless we really felt. The deception kept us precariously on the side of sanity, one whisper away from panic. I was doing this, and I knew the others were, too. I could see a guarded vulnerability in each of the kids' tired eyes that I felt in my own. If we allowed even a drop of worry to creep into our conversations, we knew we could crumble. So we kept talking, meticulously planning escape routes and filling the time with talk, refusing to give fear time to germinate and invade our thoughts—or worse, our speech. After hypothermia, panic is the worst thing that can happen to your mind and body. It uses up energy, it breaks down your will to live, and it leads you to make faulty decisions. We needed to keep our wits, to remain calm, to stay focused on living and escaping.

"OK," Guy said, breaking the three-minute silence we'd just endured. "Guess who I am." This had become a favorite time-passing game, playing "Who am I?"

Guy was wearing Kelsey's clothes from head to toe. But we didn't laugh. The rest of us were dressed the same, having split up her socks, shorts, T-shirts, and even undergarments. We were soaked when we arrived in the cave, and her Ziploc bag full of dry clothes had been our ticket out of hypothermia—that and huddling closely together in our makeshift camp. But our reprieve would likely not carry us beyond the waning daylight hours. Still, the game continued.

"Are you male?" Kelsey asked.

"Yes," Guy answered. "Keep guessing."

"Are you still alive?" Tim chimed in.

"No," Guy responded.

Guy had picked a good one. It took us a good while to figure out he was thinking of Captain George Vancouver, the eighteenth-century Englishman who had explored much of this region and after whom Vancouver Island was named.

I was thankful for games like this to fill the time, especially as we waited for Joe to return. Joe, the fifth member of our party, was our only hope. He had escaped being pummeled into the cave and had

West Coast Trail, Pacific Rim National Park, Vancouver Island, British Columbia, Canada
(Neil and Guy with Kelsey and Tim in the background)

left us to look for help. This was the third time he had headed out. Both his first and second attempts to locate the small trail that led to the main inland trail had been fruitless. And absolutely devastating for those of us in the cave. Our rescue hinged on his finding that main trail, the most likely place for him to pass other hikers, or even a ranger. When he returned not once, but twice, it took everything in us to stay positive and not despair. On top of the emotional blow, the trips had wasted valuable daylight hours for, in the dark, it would be near impossible for him to find the trail, three hours to be exact. I prayed he would be successful this third voyage, knowing we couldn't afford more lost time. He was racing the last of sunlight now.

✳ ✳ ✳

The portion of the West Coast Trail hike we'd ventured on that morning had been filled with risks. Every hike has its own dangers, but when you're hiking a boulder-strewn coastline, slipping—and falling—is a very legitimate concern. Most of the jagged rocks overlying the coastline are covered with a wet, slippery carpet of algae, and many are shaky, despite their considerable heft, able to be dislodged with the right amount and angle of pressure. Every single step must be deliberate, carefully placed, which was why we'd left so early that morning: to allow ourselves plenty of time to reach Owen Point.

We had to maneuver around Owen Point to get to our destination, and I knew we couldn't do so unless we arrived there *precisely* at low tide. I'd stayed up the night before, watching the tide come in to make sure that the tide tables I had were indeed correct for our spot on the coast. They were, so I knew I could trust the time they gave for low tide tomorrow at Owen Point. And that time was 6:30 a.m.

We made it to Owen Point that morning right at 6:30. Already the icy Pacific seawater had crept in, leaving us ten minutes tops to cross Owen Point or else we'd have to turn around and retrace our steps. We moved quickly. Crossing Owen Point, even at low tide, was dicey. In a race against the tide, we crawled and scrambled our way across the haphazard rocks as fast as we dared. By the time we finished, we were wet up to our waists. But we made it.

TWENTY ONE
The Rogue Wave

*Our first day of hiking was grueling
(Tim with Joe and Guy in the background)*

An eerie moonlike landscape welcomed us on the other side of Owen Point. Relatively flat sandstone lay in front of us, a shelf about 150 feet wide. As we began our hike along the sandstone, the Pacific waves were anything but peaceful, crashing and breaking loudly every ten seconds to our left. The waves were much bigger than what we had experienced in Port San Juan, the inlet where Thrasher Cove is located and where we'd spent the previous night, but they were at least fifty feet away, as well as below us, at the base of a good ten-foot drop-off to the shoreline on our left—much too far to be a threat this time of day. To our right, rocky cliffs towered five stories above us.

After an hour of carefully working our way along the sometimes-slick surface, we came to a wider-than-usual surge channel. Surge channels are deep, long gashes cut into a shore's soft sandstone rock. They look like mini canyons, and each time waves hit, surge channels are the epitome of chaos as huge swells of incoming ocean squeeze into their confines and crescendo to a point of angry, explosive madness. Finally the turbid waters crash against the cliffs, reverse direction, and are sucked back to sea with just as much violence.

"Hold it, guys," I said, halting the group. "This is too dangerous. We need to rope up."

I knew we couldn't simply jump as we'd done with some of the smaller channels we'd already crossed. This one was at least 5½ feet wide, with sheer rock walls that descended at least 20 feet, depending upon whether the ocean surge was coming in or going out. Algae sprinkled the flat sandstone on either side of the channel. The threat of slipping was very real.

And falling into a surge channel can be fatal. The force of seawater coming into this particular recess created a racing, roiling churn of waves traveling over 150 feet, from the coastline where the surf was pounding on our left all the way to the five-story cliff to our right. I knew we'd have to rope up to ensure a safe passage.

Joe, however, didn't hear me in time. Before I'd finished saying, "Hold it," the sprightly 6′ 4″ twenty-four-year-old was in the air, flying over the channel. He landed safely on the other side—but there was no way I was going to let the rest of us try the same foolhardy feat.

*Boulder-strewn coastline on the way to Owen Point
(Guy)*

"All right, let's get out the rope…and pass your packs to Joe." At least we'd take advantage of his leap; it would be much easier to cross the channel without the weight of our gear. We removed our backpacks, preparing to toss them to Joe. Guy, who was carrying the rope, started fishing through his pack.

CRACK!

A horrific noise, like a building imploding, echoed off the cliffs and seemed to shake the shelf on which we stood. I scanned the landscape, trying to see what had caused it, but something at my feet pulled my attention quickly downward instead. Cutting icy seawater soaked my boots and quickly swept up to my knees.

"Our gear!" Tim yelled. "Our packs are getting wet!"

The wave pushed inward, threatening to carry our packs with it, but we grabbed on and held them tight.

This doesn't make sense, I thought. *All my calculations…why are the waves hitting this far inland now?*

But I didn't have much time to think it through. Less then ten seconds later, the really big one hit—the rogue wave.

✳ ✳ ✳

A rogue wave is exactly what it sounds like—*rogue*. It is mischievous, misleading, deceptive, chaotic, heartless, selfish, and cruel. It is out to get what it wants, and take out any barrier in its path.

Including us.

After the first wave hit, I planted my feet firmly. But it didn't matter. Seconds later, the big wave swept me away, carrying my legs right out from under me.

As the water tossed me like a beach ball, I managed to keep one hand on my pack, but not for long. The weight of the wet gear was too much and dragging me down; I had to let it go.

Soon I was kicking wildly, my arms flailing, trying desperately just to find air and get my head out of the water. I was completely submerged as my waterlogged hiking clothes, boots, and raingear seemed to join forces with the rogue wave, working against every movement of my arms and legs, cruelly sucking me beneath the water's surface.

*We just made it around Owen Point at low tide
(Tim, Joe, Kelsey, Guy)*

I didn't know which way was up. I lost all sense of direction. My weight, my strength, my swimming abilities…none of these meant a thing. I was at the mercy of the turbid, roiling waters, with the water churning so powerfully about me that I swore I could feel it churning *inside* of me, deep in my gut.

I knew that the water was approximately 43°F. Yet I didn't even feel it. My senses were so inundated with input that I couldn't take it all in. Nor dare I. My concentration centered on one crucial task: to keep my head above water and breathe. Nothing else mattered. Any other thought would only interfere with my desperate attempt to stay alive.

I lost all sense of time. How long this battle went on, I have no idea. It could have lasted ten seconds, or it could have been ten minutes.

The rogue wave carried me to the foot of the cliffs, where the narrow 5 foot-plus channel had opened up to 20 feet. The fury slowed just enough, and suddenly my head popped out of the water. The water was still frantic, yet somehow I was able to catch my bearings. I gasped for breath, looking around.

As air filled my lungs, my mind expanded to let one more thought sneak in—and then EXPLODE:

My kids! Where are the kids?

At first all I could see was more schizophrenic water rumbling, cascading, rising, and falling as it pleased.

Where are they?

I continued taking in snatched gasps and gulps of watery oxygen as the angry waters continued, and finally, for the first time, I could hear. My daughter was screaming. I followed the sound of her scream and found her. She was panicked, flapping her arms wildly in an attempt to stay afloat. I knew I had to get to some sort of solid ground fast, so I could pull her out of the water.

I looked around. We were just outside the mouth of a coastal cave. Debris surrounded us. Huge tree trunks and slabs of driftwood bobbed up and down like matchsticks. Dangerous, hundred-pound matchsticks that could snap us in half. Every second we stayed there among the debris increased our chances of getting slammed against the rocks or crushed by a chunk of driftwood. And yet the rocks and the driftwood were our only hope of escape, our only "solid ground" within reach.

I spotted Guy grabbing onto a large log wedged at a 45 degree angle between two rocks, like the blade of a jackknife jammed into a tree trunk. He shimmied his way onto the log and straddled it, his body lying on top of it, his arms and legs hugging the driftwood for dear life.

I swam over to Guy, and with all the energy and strength I had left, struggled to pull myself onto the log, just as my son had done.

Kelsey swam toward the log, still screaming and crying hysterically. She was caught between two huge chunks of driftwood, either one of which could have crushed her in seconds. I reached down with my left hand and grabbed her forearm just above her left wrist.

"Don't let go!" I yelled to her. "Don't let go, Kelsey!"

She continued her frenzied screams.

I, too, was terrified, unsure that I could pull her to safety fast enough, before the logs on either side of her slammed together. I was precariously perched on my log, not in the best position to anchor myself and ensure an effective recovery. But there wasn't time to make sure everything was just right. The only option—simply grabbing hold of Kelsey's arm and pulling her onto the log—could very well mean my own falling back into the water. But it was the only option.

I gripped her arm tight and pulled, adrenaline coursing through my veins. I don't know how, but it worked, and she was by my side, still hysterical, but safe. As I held her tight, we watched the two logs collide, knowing she had escaped their crushing impact by only a few seconds.

By this point, Tim had found the log, as well. I comforted Kelsey as Tim clawed his way to safety.

Clinging to that log like monkeys to a tree, we were safe but only temporarily. We couldn't remain, but we had few options. We had the surge channel in front of us, 20 foot cliffs on either side, and a huge coastal cave to our backs. If we wanted to live—if we wanted to avoid being smashed to pieces or sucked out to sea—we had to find a way into that cave.

The waves continued crashing powerfully around us, but only every 10 seconds or so. We realized that, in the 10 second intervals, we could leapfrog our way across huge rocks that were anchored to the ocean floor, rocks whose tips were exposed like icebergs whenever the waves receded.

We started working toward the cave, scampering across the huge rocks and then pausing whenever a wave hit, gripping tight to whatever we could find—a rock or piece of driftwood—so as not to be swept away. In the lulls between waves, we'd move on to the next rock. It was slow work, but we made it to the cave. Once inside, we faced our next obstacle: scaling its sides to get out of the water's reach, a good four stories up. The first two stories were treacherous rock-climbing, much worse than any of the boulders we'd navigated earlier that day. The rocks were massive, almost 6 feet wide in all directions. And they were wet, making them dangerously slick.

The next few stories required clawing our way across chunks of driftwood wedged awkwardly into the sandstone cave's walls. We were completely enervated. The frigid waters, the beating from the waves, the two-story boulder climb…and all that on top of an already strenuous hike. Eventually we found our way to a four-story high driftwood perch that would become our home for the next 9 hours.

❊ ❊ ❊

"Can you imagine if Joe hadn't jumped?" I asked. "All five of us would be stuck in here—and who would be out looking for help?"

Up there with "Who am I?" this was another of our favorite time-passing games in the cave—counting our blessings. Yes, we were stuck in a coastal cave. But a crazy array of fortuitous happenings had ensured that our situation was far from hopeless.

Such as the fact that Kelsey had tossed her pack to Joe before the rogue wave hit so that it and all its contents—clothes and a sleeping bag—were dry enough to use.

An eerie moonlike landscape

Or the fact that we'd had our packs off when the rogue wave hit and swept us into the surge channel. If we'd had our packs on, we would have been dragged down into the channel.

Or the fact that we'd been swept into a cave tall enough and equipped with enough footholds and old driftwood for us to climb high and avoid the rising tide.

Or the fact that we'd been swept into the cave at all. If the surge channel waves had been receding when the rogue wave hit, we would have been sucked out to sea to certain death.

Or the fact that Joe had not been swept into the surge channel and was able to go look for help.

Or the discovery that maybe there was another way out. Kelsey had found a back entrance to the cave in her own series of serendipitous events. She had had to pee, so we had helped her down the dangerous descent of the cave's walls so that she could find a private place below. Moments later, we heard her yelling excitedly.

"Guys! Guys! I think I see light."

We made the descent ourselves and joined her when she had finished. Sure enough, there was light shining through what appeared to be a back entrance to the cave, an entrance we never would have found had Kelsey not chosen that particular spot to pee.

It was a sizable opening, and we quickly realized this was our best bet for an escape. At that point the tide was too high, but we realized, once the water receded some more, we could probably gather at the base of what was essentially a pit beneath that huge hole and find a way up the cavern walls and through the opening.

✳ ✳ ✳

It was 5 o'clock, and Joe had returned to the sandstone shelf outside the cave. He still could not see us, or we him, but we could yell to each other. He had ropes in hand, retrieved from an abandoned ranger's cabin he had broken into by busting through the window with an axe he had found. Ropes were essential to our escape, and I was grateful for his find.

He yelled down to us that he had met a German couple hiking on the trail who promised to try and find a phone to call for help. It

*A surge channel, but not the wider-than-usual
surge channel
(Joe)*

was nice to know there were others out there trying to locate help of some sort, but I didn't let that derail our escape attempts. As far as I was concerned, getting out of that cave was up to us. I'd spent most of my life learning that I was my most reliable ally; the idea of waiting around for outside help to show up never even crossed my mind.

We sprang into action to implement our latest escape plan. It followed a dangerous escape route with the potential for falling and injury. And because it involved getting wet, it posed an increased risk of hypothermia at every step. But it was our only known possibility for escape.

We'd already exhausted all other options. Initially, we considered climbing out the front entrance of the cave. This would have required Joe stationing himself at the top of the mouth of the cave and lowering a rope down for us to scale. But the ledge above the cave's mouth turned out to be nothing more than a very shallow lip. There was nowhere for Joe to stand, or us for that matter, once we'd scaled the rope.

We had also considered the "low-tide option." This involved waiting until low tide and then finding our way back out to the opening in front of the cave and somehow scaling the 20 foot walls on the sides. But low tide turned out to be not low enough. Even at low tide, the water level outside the cave's opening was still too high to consider safely scaling the walls.

And so here we were, climbing down and through four stories of driftwood logs wedged into the cave's walls like giant pick-up sticks until each of us reached water level, so that we could attempt our third escape plan, through the back opening of the cave.

A slip or fall at this step would have been easy to make, and the consequences disastrous. In my nervous state, I couldn't help but envision my daughter losing her tenuous grip on a narrow piece of driftwood and falling and bouncing from one huge piece of driftwood onto another log…and then another, and another, all the way down four stories until finally she fell into the water.

Stay in the moment, Neil. Focus, focus.

Drawing by Tim Kniffin, ocean perspective

We made the descent safely. Onto the next step: wading through the icy water, up to our shins, until we made it to the base of the pit where Joe would lower a rope for us to climb. This part of the escape was risky because it exposed us to the cold water. If our rescue didn't work, we would find ourselves battling hypothermia again—this time through the cold dark night.

We slogged through the water to the base of the opening, a perfectly round 100 foot diameter depression in the earth. Steep six-story walls surrounded all sides of the monstrous hole. It was impressive… and daunting. Algae covered the walls. Even with the rope, we realized that scaling the walls would still require Herculean strength. And patience. Inching up those slippery sides would be slow, hard work.

Hang in there, Neil. Don't lose focus…

The tide was coming in, filling the rocky bottom of the pit with water. We didn't have much time before the water would be too high for us to be here. We gathered and looked up to Joe, who had rappelled down to a dried-up waterfall four stories above where we stood. This was the first time we could actually *see* Joe since we'd been pounded into the cave.

It felt good to stand after sitting scrunched up on driftwood for so long. And it was refreshing to look up and see the sky. We could actually see daylight through the patchwork of tree branches hanging over the opening above.

Joe tied together the two ropes, end to end, to make an extra long rope. He then tied one end to a tree and lowered the rope down the cliff. The plan was to shimmy up the rope, hand over hand, for the full four stories.

We quickly realized it couldn't be done that way. After battling the cold and merciless waves in the surge channel and shivering in a cave for nine hours, we were in no shape to pull our weight up the entire length of a four-story rope. We needed footholds. There were no footholds on the cave's vertical walls, and the handful of ledges that did exist were just inches wide and filled with slippery algae.

I asked Joe to tie footholds in the rope. He did so, but the rope was long enough to allow only two stories worth of footholds. It would

Drawing by Tim Kniffin, helicopter perspective

have to do: a four-story-long rope with footholds on only the bottom two stories. With night quickly approaching, we were running out of time and had no viable alternative. We had to push forward.

I sent Guy, the most athletic, up first. Scaling the rope was difficult, even for him. The footholds were every 12 inches, requiring big, stretching steps. On top of that, the footholds were floppy; Guy had to manually open each one before placing his foot into it. And once he'd finished the first two stories with footholds, the most tiring work was still ahead: shimmying up the rope, hand over hand, until he reached the top—no footholds, no walls to push off of, nothing to rely on but his upper body strength.

He made it to the top, an incredible feat. I seriously doubted that the rest of us would be able to do the same, but we had no other options. We had to give it a go and improvise along the way if needed.

Kelsey was next. She moved more slowly than Guy, but she made it up the first two stories with footholds. There was no way she was going to be able to scale the last two stories, so Guy and Joe decided to pull her up. The rope swung wildly from side to side with each yank, with poor Kelsey gripping to the rope for dear life. When they finally pulled her to the top, she had to claw her way over the edge to safety. It was tense, but she made it.

Next, Tim readied for his escape. He had tremendous difficulty scaling even the first two stories with footholds. He flopped all over the place. When he started on the more treacherous half of the climb without footholds, he struggled even more, to the point of actually losing his grip. I held my breath and watched in agony as my best friend's son fell a full two stories into the water below. He was shaken, scraped up, but fortunately not seriously injured.

The tide was coming in at this point, the water now at our thighs. I had run out of escape plans. This had been our only option, and it clearly wasn't going to work for Tim and me. There was no way I was going to try the climb and leave Tim there by himself. As the water continued rising, I realized he and I would simply have to scale our way back into the cave before the water got even higher. We would

Drawing by Tim Kniffin, horizontal perspective

have to spend another night there in the cave on the driftwood and tackle our escape tomorrow.

I opened my mouth to tell Tim the plan, but a noise interrupted me. A familiar sound. The sound of a rotor. Of a helicopter!

They found us!

But then, as the helicopter's *chop-chop-chop* grew quieter, I realized maybe they hadn't found us. Maybe they couldn't see us. The tide was still coming in, and the water was now knee high.

Kelsey yelled down. "Dad, what's that noise?"

Tim asked simultaneously, "Neil, what is that?"

I yelled back to Kelsey, "It's a helicopter!"

The noise grew again. The helicopter was circling back. Suddenly, I could actually see it through the limbs and leaves above. But then, just as quickly, the noise and the helicopter were past us again.

Did they see us? We can't lose this chance!

I cupped my hands over my mouth and yelled up the cavern walls. "Joe! Guy!" They peered down into the cave. "Can you run out to the sandstone shelf and wave down the helicopter? I don't think they can see us here with all the trees. Can you do that?"

I hoped it wasn't too late, that the helicopter hadn't already given up and left the area.

Twenty minutes later, I heard the chopper again. The water had crept above our thighs by that point. Then a man appeared on the narrow ledge four stories above us.

And to me, from where I stood 40 feet below his perch, he looked like Superman. He wore a one-piece Coast Guard dry suit that made him look extra muscular, a little like Popeye. The suit was orange and black, with red interspersed.

My initial elation at seeing my own personal Superman was quickly deflated when I saw his reaction as he looked at Tim and me in the bottom of our 100 foot-diameter pit, with the water now almost midway up our thighs.

He let out a huge sigh. It was clear he had no idea how to get us out of there. He was stumped, absolutely dumbfounded. But he was not

Drawing by Tim Kniffin, view from the cave

giving up. I saw his mind working overtime as he calculated a way to get Tim and me out of that hole.

Finally, after his initial moments of exasperation and indecision, it was clear that Superman had a plan. He grabbed his mobile radio and asked his cohorts in the chopper to lower some additional ropes and harnesses.

He returned to the ledge four stories above us with plenty of rope—a thick, long coil—which he tied together. This time the rope had plenty of length. But no footholds.

Instead, at the end of the rope was a red shoulder harness, which we were supposed to strap on. Then he, Joe, and Guy would haul us up the four stories to safety. The harness didn't look like anything special. At 5 inches wide, 2 inches deep, and 3 feet long, the piece of foam looked and felt like nothing more than a waistline life preserver.

"I can't believe that can hold us," I said. "What do you think, Tim?"

Tim nodded in agreement, but there was no time for conjecture. Superman began yelling instructions down to Tim, who would go first, on how to secure the harness around his chest and under his shoulders, holding on to the rope above his head. Tim put the device around his shoulders. I remained skeptical that it could hold him. At 6'3" and 230 pounds, Tim was a big 28 year-old.

Next, Superman instructed Tim to "rappel backwards" up the cliff, to essentially walk up the cliff at a position perpendicular to the rocks. Somehow this would give Superman, Guy, and Joe the leverage they needed to pull Tim up the four stories to safety.

Tim began his ascent. He leaned backward while Joe, Guy, and Superman held the rope to prevent him from falling on his back in the water. Tim placed one foot on the rock-lined walls, then the other foot. He was in the right position, but could he hold it and climb up the four slippery stories?

On only his second step, Tim lost his footing. There was too much algae on the rocks for him to get a good grip with his feet. He slipped and fell. But the rope, with Superman, Joe, and Guy on the other end, kept his upper body out of the water. Tim hung there, his feet dangling in the water.

TWENTY ONE
THE ROGUE WAVE

The next thing I heard was Superman yelling to Joe and Guy, "Heave, *HO!*" and they began pulling Tim out of the hole. It was not a smooth, graceful rescue. It took about 10 minutes for them to pull him up. Tim looked liked a beached whale, banging against the rocks on each yank of the rope, but he made it. Eventually he was safely out of the cave with the others, and Superman lowered the rope back down for my escape.

I was anxious to get out of that cave and onto dry land with my family. I set my jaw, gritted my teeth, and focused all my strength toward scaling that wall. I quickly discovered that sheer determination sometimes just isn't enough, that physical realities demand a revised plan. I lost my footing on the slippery walls, just as Tim had, and the guys above pulled me laboriously to the top as they had with Tim.

Eventually, I, too, was safe. We had all been rescued.

A few moments later, as we waited to be lifted into the helicopter, we saw approximately a half-dozen boats on the water, some U.S. and Canadian Coast Guard, some National Oceanic and Atmospheric Administration (NOAA), some privately owned.

All of them were looking for bodies. Our bodies.

※ ※ ※

The amount of wind a helicopter creates is unbelievable. As we stood there on the sandstone shelf beneath the deafening chopper, it took everything in us just to stay standing. Superman pointed at me in a take-charge manner that I didn't dare argue with. I was to be airlifted first. Period.

They lowered a see-through basket with wire mesh around it, and I climbed in. As I huddled up inside, the basket rose, spinning in the chopper's wind the whole way up. At the top, another Coastguardsman held the basket while I climbed out and ordered me into the corner of the helicopter. I moved to where he pointed and sat on the floor.

Kelsey was next. When she reached the top, she climbed out of the basket, joined me in the corner, and crawled under my arm. And then she just lost it. She sobbed uncontrollably, releasing all the pent-up emotion of the painfully tense ordeal. We were finally safe.

Because of space limitations on the helicopter, it took two trips to get all of us out of there: Guy, Kelsey, and me on the first trip, Tim and Joe on the next. They took us to Port Renfrew, the southernmost trailhead, where we were met with a congregation of EMTs, reporters, and local townspeople. After the EMTs checked us out, we were taken to a motel, where we cleaned up and changed into dry clothes provided for us.

Finally, around 10 p.m., we headed to a local diner that had stayed open late, just for us.

During our 9 hour ordeal, all we'd had to eat and drink were two granola bars and two cups of water. And that was for us to share, between the four of us. Understandably, we were famished. We all ordered the same celebratory meal: clam chowder, Caesar salad, hamburger, fries, apple pie, and ice cream.

We couldn't stop smiling. Our bodies were exhausted, but the relief we felt after surviving the most harrowing experience of our lives was sweeter than anything we'd ever tasted.

As the meal arrived, I said grace.

"Lord," I began, "we realize we have a lot to be thankful for. We know that You have been with us today, or else we would not be here now. We could have been swept out to sea instead of into the cave where You protected us. Kelsey's pack could have gotten soaked like the rest of ours instead of staying dry so that we would have clothes to wear. Joe could have been swept into the channel along with the rest of us instead of escaping the waves like he did so that he could find help for us. And Tim and I could have been stuck in that cave another night instead of being rescued by the Coast Guard."

I glanced up and saw Kelsey wiping a tear off her cheek.

"Lord, we know You've been looking out for us. We know that it simply isn't our time to leave yet and that You want us here for a reason. Thank you, Lord. Amen."

❋ ❋ ❋

I still can't think of what we went through that day without getting choked up. It was such an intense, uncertain, emotion-filled experience.

I'd been through trials in my life before. Working my tail off to make the grade in school when others insisted I was incapable of doing so. Interviewing for jobs when those I was up against were clearly more qualified. Even learning to live—and play sports—as if from the start, after losing an eye.

But nothing compares to what I experienced that day on Vancouver Island. With my life—and, more important, my kids' lives—on the line, I faced the single most difficult, most frightening, most harrowing challenge of my life. I probably couldn't have survived had I not met and surmounted earlier challenges. They had all prepared me for the big one. They'd shown me that my physical capabilities were far greater than most believed. And more important, they'd taught me that my mental state determined my success. Perseverance, in the end, determined whether one survives or not. I'd internalized that lesson I'd learned over and over again about what it meant to stick it out, to stay the course, to finish strong. Without my résumé of obstacles "passed," I wouldn't have had a level enough head to get us out of that cave alive.

Maybe the real blessing wasn't simply getting out of the cave. It was also knowing I'd faced and overcome a lifetime full of challenges so that I had the resources when I needed them the most—to save the lives of the ones most dear to me.

Stay focused, Neil. Stay focused…

Epilogue

Today, at an age when many individuals are thinking about retirement—after serving as the Seattle, Oakland, and Los Angeles Metro transportation leader and after founding and selling Flexcar, the award-winning car-sharing company—I've just begun writing the next chapter of my life, a chapter called the "Edge Foundation."

Writing this chapter has been unavoidable. It's as if life put the pen in my hand and said, "Get to work, Neil! Write!" It started in 2000, when my son Guy was diagnosed with ADHD. Right after that my daughter was also diagnosed with ADHD. The doctor said it was hereditary, and I knew then and there that I must have ADHD, too. I'd seen their struggles, and they were familiar; I'd experienced them myself. Poor grades. Problems with time management. Lack of focus. Impulsivity. And, worst of all, low self-esteem. But we found many ways of creatively coping, and despite the challenges, we continued to press on and thrive.

Guy and Kelsey had both been tested extensively in high school at the recommendation of a teacher. But during Kelsey's senior year of high school, she had to be tested again for her condition in order to be considered for special learning accommodations in college. The tests were administered one day a week over the course of three weeks.

On the last day, when I went to pick up Kelsey from her testing, the psychologist drew a bell curve on a chalkboard. The bell curve, he explained, represented the IQs of all 18 year-olds in the United States, with the expanded center representing the largest numbers, which were of average intelligence. He asked Kelsey where she thought she fell along the curve. Obviously uncomfortable, she finally pointed to the left side and said, "About in the middle, a little below average." She was wrong. The psychologist set us both straight. Although my daughter fell into the 20th percentile for reading, spelling, and math, her overall IQ was way above the 90th percentile and her verbal and non-verbal reasoning scores were off the charts.

I'll never forget what happened next. As we left the doctor's office, Kelsey looked at me, jumped into the air, gave me a high five, and said, "Dad, I'm brilliant." No words had ever meant so much to me, or to her, and nothing was truer.

Two years later, when Kelsey was home on break from college, she said to me, "Dad, of all the things you've done for me, the most valuable and most appreciated is the gift you gave me of my own personal coach." I'd become familiar with the practice of using personal coaches during my decades in the corporate world, and I'd decided to hire personal coaches for myself and my kids, as a way to help us all stay focused, reflect on our success and failures, and monitor our progress on academic, personal, and professional goals. Initially Kelsey had been skeptical; she didn't seem to understand the benefit of using personal coaches. Yet here she was singling out coaching as the most significant to her of all the methods I'd tried to help my kids deal with ADHD—more important than the spell-checking, voice-recognition, and verbal dictation software; the specially colored notebooks and specially designed wristwatches; the medications and complicated diets and sleep regimens.

Not much later, right after I sold my company following a successful corporate and public sector career, Kelsey asked me what I was going to do next with my life. I told her that I had no idea, that I was looking for my next passion. But my daughter had already figured it out for me. "Dad," she said, "I know what you ought to do. You ought to do for other kids what you did for me and Guy."

I couldn't speak I was so overcome. Kelsey had seen my future. It was so simple, so powerful. I decided right then to start the Edge Foundation to help young people with ADHD realize their potential and their passion. And I decided that the Foundation strategy would be centered on providing each young person with a professional coach. Today the Foundation is under way, and I look forward to seeing it grow as we help more and more young men and young women students with ADHD.

When Guy, Kelsey, Tim, and I were swept up in that rogue wave in 2007, the Edge Foundation was in its incipient stages. That experience strengthened my resolve to continue with creating the Foundation. It was as if that near-death experience confirmed for me that *this*, creating the Edge Foundation, was precisely what I was supposed to be doing right here, right now. I sensed, like I'd never sensed before, that it was my calling.

In many ways, ADHD saved our lives that day in the cave. The characteristic inattention of ADHD transforms into hyperfocus in times of crisis, and that is precisely what happened for Guy, Kelsey, Tim, and me. Each one of us has ADHD, and I am convinced that that is what allowed us to concentrate so intensely on creating an escape plan and ultimately to not despair during our 10 grueling hours inside that cave. It is my hope that the Edge Foundation will help others do the same—to realize their full potential, to find their passion, and to achieve great things even amidst life's struggles.

About the Author

Neil Peterson's professional career has two very different chapters to it, but with a common entrepreneurial theme.

The first is the business entrepreneurial chapter. His most recent business success was the highly acclaimed Flexcar, which Neil founded in 1999. Flexcar, which merged in 2007 with Zipcar—called "time-share automobiles" by some—operates in many cities across the country, providing an answer to Americans' desire to reduce their reliance on foreign oil; meet environmental, carbon reduction, and global warming goals; and make our cities more livable.

Flexcar and Neil have been featured by various national media outlets, including *TIME Magazine, Fortune Small Business, USA Today, The Wall Street Journal, The Washington Post, The New York Times, NPR, ABC World News Tonight,* and *Good Morning America.* Neil's achievements with Flexcar have also received numerous awards, including the 2005 "Top Brand with a Conscience," the 2004 "Sustainable Community Outstanding Leadership Award," the 2004 "It's Not Easy Being Green Award," the 2002 "Clean Air Award," the 2002

"Spirit of the Northwest Award," the "2001 Environmental Excellence Award," and the 2001 "Vision 2020 Award."

A self-confessed serial entrepreneur, Neil has founded four other businesses and has been the CEO, COO, or CFO of five additional companies, and worked as a consultant for Booz, Allen & Hamilton.

The second chapter of Neil's professional career is as a public servant. He is best known for serving eleven years as executive director for the public transportation systems (the Metros) in the Los Angeles, San Francisco's East Bay, and Seattle metropolitan areas. Previously he served as a city manager and worked for two U.S. congressmen, two state governments, and the anti-poverty program.

In these roles he has received numerous awards. While serving as CEO of Los Angeles' Metro, he received the prestigious Tranny Award for "Manager of the Year" presented by the California Transportation Foundation; the "Clean Air Award" for "Individual Excellence in Leadership in Government," presented by the Southern California Air Quality Management District; the "Visionary Leadership Award," presented by UCLA's Graduate School of Architecture and Urban Planning; and the Urban Mass Transit Administration's "Administrators Award for Outstanding Public Service."

While Neil served as its CEO, Seattle's Metro received APTA's national "Outstanding Large Transit Agency in the U.S. Award." Similarly, while serving as Los Angeles' LACTC's CEO, the agency received APTA's "National Management Innovation Award," as well as the Women's Transportation Seminar's (WTS) "Employer of the Year Award," presented for providing opportunities for women in the transportation field. He also was selected by *TIME Magazine* as one of the "100 Newsmakers of Tomorrow."

What is not so well known is Neil's work with and passion for people with disabilities in our society. While serving as COO of the Department of Social and Health Services (DSHS) supervising 10,000 employees, Neil was responsible for running Washington state's programs for individuals with physical and mental disabilities. He served on the board of a nonprofit agency helping those who are blind and have visual impairments. At Seattle Metro he was responsible for making Metro the first large transit agency in the country to adopt and successfully implement a full accessibility policy for people with disabilities on all Metro buses. For this, he received an award from the Disabled American Veterans.

Additionally, Neil previously served as vice president of the Edna McConnell Clark Foundation, whose focus is advancing opportunities for low-income youth.

The father of two children with a learning disability and attention deficit/hyperactivity disorder (ADHD), Neil himself has dyslexia and ADHD. Neil and his kids have been featured in ADDitude magazine.

He also has what might by some be viewed as a physical handicap—he has only one eye. Yet he is able to carry a 7 handicap in golf without having any depth perception.

Most recently Neil is the founder, chairman, and CEO of the Edge Foundation, whose mission is to help young students who have ADHD realize their potential and their passion by providing them with their own personal coach.

Neil was educated at Williams College in Massachusetts and received his master's degree from the Woodrow Wilson School of Public and International Affairs at Princeton University. Having taught courses at Rutgers University and the University of Washington, he currently speaks frequently at various events. This publication is his first book, and he recently was selected as a finalist in the Pacific Northwest Writers Association's annual contest.

An inveterate cyclist, hiker, golfer, ballroom dancer, and ice hockey player, Neil lives on a houseboat in Seattle, and his top priority in his life is being a great father.

Do you have your own stories? Stories where tenacity played a crucial role? Stories where perseverance powered you through? With your responses we are planning on putting together an anthology of individual stories of perseverance and tenacity. Please submit your stories to neil@neilpeterson.com